Wall-to-Wall History

Martin Wildgoose, who discovered the multi-period walls at Roystone, sitting on the foundations of a Romano-British wall (photo: Richard Hodges)

Wall-to-Wall History

The story of Roystone Grange

Richard Hodges

Duckworth

First published in 1991 by
Gerald Duckworth & Co. Ltd.
The Old Piano Factory
43 Gloucester Crescent, London NW1 7DY

ISBN 0 7156 2342 7

British Library Cataloguing in Publication Data

Hodges, Richard *1952–*
    Wall-to-wall history : the story of Roystone Grange.
    1. Derbyshire (England). Archaeology
    I. Title
    942.11

    ISBN 0–7156–2342–7

Photoset in North Wales by
Derek Doyle & Associates, Mold, Clwyd.
Printed in Great Britain by
Ebenezer Baylis & Son Ltd, Worcester.

Contents

To Peggy & John

Preface

No study seems more liable to draw off the mind from serious matters,
than that of Antiquities – it has the dangerously plausible character of
being a harmless pursuit; but it seems scarcely ever to call forth a
serious reflection from its votaries.
William Bateman in a letter to Joseph Hunter, January 1829.

Archaeology can no longer be carried out by the lone adventurer. Field
projects, such as that at Roystone Grange, are the sum of contributions
by many archaeologists. In writing this book, therefore, I am reminded
of a small army of students from Sheffield University, as well as many
friends. In particular, I am grateful to the supervisors of the many
excavations and surveys – Gillian Clarke, Cathy Coutts, Mark
Edmonds, John Moreland, Elaine Morris, Andy Myres, Simon Probert,
Julian Thomas and David Wilkinson – and to my colleagues, some of
whom contributed to the project, and all of whom supported it: Graeme
Barker, Keith Branigan, John Collis, Andrew Fleming, David
Gilbertson, Cliff Samson and Robin Torrence.

I owe many of the ideas in the book to debates and discussions at
Roystone with a large number of archaeologists. I recall my debt to
Pauline Beswick, Don Bramwell, David Crossley, Clive Gamble, Clive
Hart, Steve Moorhouse, Jean Le Patourel, Don Spratt, Jonathon
Wager and the late Percy Heathcote.

The Peak District National Park has taken an active interest in our
activities since the beginning of the project, and is now co-sponsor of it.
For this happy state of affairs I owe much to Ken Smith, the Park's
archaeologist, who has promoted the project with selfless determin-
ation. I also thank George Challenger, Suzanne Fletcher, Hugh
Gunton, Ken Parker and Diane Tranter. The project has been
supported by funds from the Robert Kiln Trust, the Prehistoric Society,
Sheffield City Museums, Sheffield University and the Society of
Antiquaries. I am grateful to all these institutions, and trust that the
results live up to their expectations.

Like the project itself, the writing of the book has been a
collaborative effort. I am grateful to my wife Debbie, David Twigge,
Ken Smith and Martin Wildgoose for commenting on the text, and to
Pauline Beswick, Ray Manley and Derrick Riley for many of the fine
photographs. Barry Vincent prepared the line drawings with his

vii

customary skill.

I shall always remember the project for the sublime tranquillity of the place, the often dramatic nature of the landscape and the companionship of John and Peggy Duncan, Margaret Poulter, David Twigge, and in particular Martin Wildgoose. This book belongs to them all; but most of all to John and Peggy who persuaded me to visit Roystone Grange in the first place.

R.H.

Introduction

It is in the darkish Midlands, on the rim of a steep deep valley, looking over darkish, folded hills – exactly the navel of England, and feels exactly that.

D.H. Lawrence to Catherine Carswell, describing
Middleton-by-Wirksworth in April 1918.

A Sunday in March 1978. John Duncan came racing across the carpark, ignoring the drizzle in his enthusiasm to tell me that a skeleton had been unearthed at Roystone Grange. Could we make a detour to see it, he asked, as it wasn't far from several of the other sites we were due to visit on our end-of-session field-trip? It seemed a good idea. My tutor at university had urged me to seek out a grange to investigate when I moved to the lectureship at Sheffield. Granges, he had advised, were archaeologically rich and invariably tied into the main thread of English history.

The drizzle turned to driving rain as we left Bakewell. Low cloud lay like a blanket over the Miner's Standard at Winster as we came up onto the White Peak plateau. We continued south towards Ashbourne before branching off to Parwich and on to Ballidon. The rain was turning to sleet when we paused to inspect the deserted medieval village at Ballidon. Nobody wanted to venture across the earthworks or to see inside the lonely chapel, so John led our convoy of cars through the gorge cut by the huge quarry which has consumed the southern face of the White Peak plateau beyond Ballidon. For a moment we wondered if we had made a mistake, but John seemed certain of the direction. Beyond the quarry he found a grassy track that wound its way up a steep dry valley until we approached a strange chapel-like building, and then, only half visible in the dark misty light, Roystone Grange Farm. Beside the building John got out, waded through the mud churned up by cows and told us that we must pass through the farmyard to the dairy. This we did, increasingly aware of the fierce weather and the eerie isolation of the place.

At the dairy we were met by a lean, rugged-looking farmer with a cap that had rubbed the flanks of many a cow in his milking parlour. He seemed pleased to see us. First he showed us a black-burnished pot – possibly a funerary urn – that a friend had given him. I pronounced it probably of Roman date. Then, ignoring the elements, we trailed after

1

1. Panorama of Roystone Grange (photo: Ray Manley).

him around the sides of the dairy to inspect a new cutting he had been making for a modern parlour. His cows had puddled the ground into a paddy-field of liquid mud, and we were all clearly conscious that we couldn't have chosen a worse day for the trip. Exposed in the rough edge of the bulldozer cutting lay the glistening, cream-coloured bones of a skeleton. Only the trunk survived, embedded in a layer of clean white sand which a geomorphologist told us was a dew-pond. Everyone stared at the bones – later we were to learn from J.T. Chesterman, a retired Home Office pathologist, that they belonged to a young woman aged 18-24 years with a strong right arm.

Was this a medieval burial, I wondered, recalling my tutor's advice?
To find out I wandered along the bulldozer cutting, followed faithfully
by the group. To my astonishment a clean darkish layer, a few
centimetres below the sodden turf, contained potsherds that were
undeniably of Roman date. The big fragments of cooking vessels
obviously belonged to a homestead that must lie close by. So, as John
often relates, I paid scant heed to the driving rain and led my gaggle of
armchair archaeologists up the slope. There beyond all doubt lay a fine
house platform of a well-known Romano-British type. Beyond it were
traces of a walled enclosure, the last indications of a farmyard
constructed eighteen hundred years ago. The farmer and I became

2. Students excavating at Roystone (photo: Ray Manley).

engaged in an enthusiastic conversation about the archaeology here, blissfully unaware that the sleety rain had driven my companions back through the mud to the warmth of their cars. The farmer, it became clear, was delighted that we had troubled to come. Would we return to excavate?

*

The discovery of Roystone is etched on my mind. But the past ten years of working there have not been without incident. We returned in driving snow the following day and excavated the skeleton. In the conditions our efforts were far from exemplary, but the farmer was

4

pleased. It so happened that Derrick Riley, an honorary lecturer in Sheffield University and a celebrated air photographer who had learned his craft as a bomber pilot in the war, chanced to fly over Roystone in early May. His photographs revealed traces of Roman-period fields and many other intriguing earthworks.

So we returned to Roystone and began a friendship with this engaging farmer. His name is David Twigge, and Peakland archaeology will be forever indebted to him for his kindness, enthusiasm and good humour. David allowed us to explore the house platform associated with the skeleton and anything else we might find in the valley. This was to be the happy pattern of the project for the next ten years.

The first group of Sheffield undergraduates were bussed out to the farm in late June, and encountered the memorable mixture of idyllic sunny days and wintry storms that characterise the White Peak in summer. The trial excavation showed convincingly that the homestead merited a full-scale investigation. In July we uncovered the entire platform with a team of Americans. But once again the weather proved appalling. Indeed we were close to abandoning the enterprise one Sunday, and spent a long, rather depressed lunchtime in the Sycamore at Parwich wondering what to do. When we returned, Roystone was shrouded in mist. The team, however, were philosophical and set off to their various trenches.

At that moment a young man appeared out of the mist, careless of the driving rain, and advanced towards us up the track. He introduced himself as Martin Wildgoose, saying that he had been helping on archaeological digs for years. He was a farmer at Kniveton, but the weather was too bad to cut the hay – so could he join us? I stared in disbelief and said yes. Without doubt the project changed at that moment. Martin is an excellent excavator and his enthusiasm brought an air of excitement to our investigations. Above all, as a farmer he has a remarkable empathy with landscapes. Realising this, I encouraged him to map the earthworks and walls in the valley. He began that July in pouring rain, and continued off and on until 1986, when he submitted his study for the British Archaeological Awards and won the Pitt-Rivers prize to become, in effect, archaeologist of the year.

Each June for the past ten years we have run excavations with first-year students from Sheffield, camping in the meadow below the farmhouse. Gradually we have assembled a picture of the place which makes it seem exceptional. Three hundred students have come to associate Roystone with their first taste of archaeology. From the beginning, however, we intended to use the project not only to instruct our students, but also to bring practical archaeology to a wider public. In 1980 we issued a booklet describing a trail round the archaeology of the farm. That June the landscape architect Jonathon Wager discovered us sheltering from the rain. He quizzed us about the project and wrote about it in his report to the Peak District National Park on the conservation of historic landscapes. This triggered the Park's interest in Roystone. In 1984, in collaboration with Sheffield University, they sponsored an archaeological trail round Roystone Grange. The success of this trail persuaded the Park that the important parts of the farm should be purchased when David Twigge retired. This they did in 1987.

The purpose of this book is to bring together the results of ten years' research at Roystone and its implications for the long history of the White Peak. It summarises the scientific reports that will appear separately. It also summarises the painstaking and imaginative investigations of Martin Wildgoose, whom I regard as a co-author. Our work was made possible by the generosity and enthusiasm of David Twigge, to whom we have dedicated our full reports. This book, we feel, belongs to Peggy and John who urged us to make a detour on that wet Sunday in March 1978, and who have shown us incomparable friendship in the decade since that trip.

1

Interrogating the Landscape

The word 'palimpsest' has often been used to describe the English landscape, implying that it is the result of the superimposition of one set of features on another throughout time; but the reality is somewhat different. The history of settlement in England is not just the story of man's adaptation to dull geographical determinants, grinding social pressures, inevitable economic change or anything else that geographers, historians and archaeologists tell us. It is all these but it is much more. Most of all it is a wonderful, richly coloured, whirling kaleidoscope of movement and change. If we appreciate this then we may understand our past, present and perhaps even our future.

Christopher Taylor, *Village and Farmstead* (1982)

The Derbyshire Dome, or the White Peak, is the limestone heartland of the Peak District National Park. It forms the southern end of the Pennine spine, bounded to the east, west and north by high gritstone moors. To the south lies the Midlands – champion country, as medieval topographers described it, with its swelling hills muffled with hedgerows, long meadow-grass and thick corn. The Dome is best known for its stark beauty and ecological riches. Yet clearly imprinted upon these pastures is a palimpsest of English history that offers the curious a 'richly coloured, whirling kaleidoscope of movement and change'. These impressions on the landscape have barely been noticed until recently. To interpret them we need a point of reference – somewhere that echoes the rhythms of Peakland history, and embodies the spirit of six thousand years. This point is Roystone Grange.

Roystone Grange is a typical hill farm. The farmhouse itself is situated half-way up a dry valley at 283 metres above sea level at the southern edge of the White Peak, overlooked by high pastures stretching up to Minninglow to the east and the craggy hill known as Roystone Rocks to the west. The farm covers nearly 400 acres, and with its neighbours, Minninglow Grange and Ballidon Moor Farm, forms the northern, upland half of Ballidon parish. Oats and root-crops will grow in the dry valley, but only with difficulty on the hilltops. Cattle tend to poach the ground in the winter, thereby impeding the uniform growth of spring grass. The land is ideal, however, for sheep.

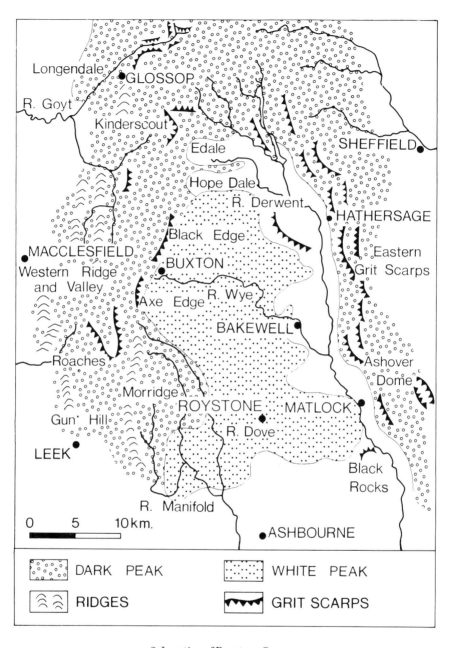

DARK PEAK		WHITE PEAK	
RIDGES		GRIT SCARPS	

3. Location of Roystone Grange.

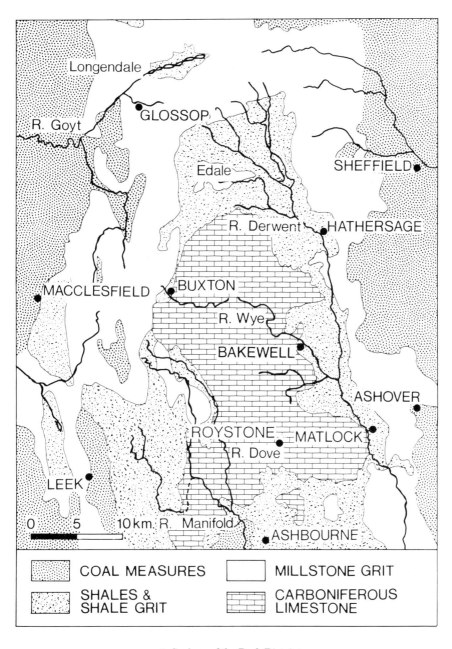

Labels within the map:

Longendale

R. Goyt

GLOSSOP

Edale

SHEFFIELD

R. Derwent

HATHERSAGE

MACCLESFIELD

BUXTON

R. Wye

BAKEWELL

ASHOVER

ROYSTONE

MATLOCK

R. Dove

LEEK

0 5 10 km R. Manifold

ASHBOURNE

COAL MEASURES

MILLSTONE GRIT

SHALES &
SHALE GRIT

CARBONIFEROUS
LIMESTONE

4. Geology of the Peak District.

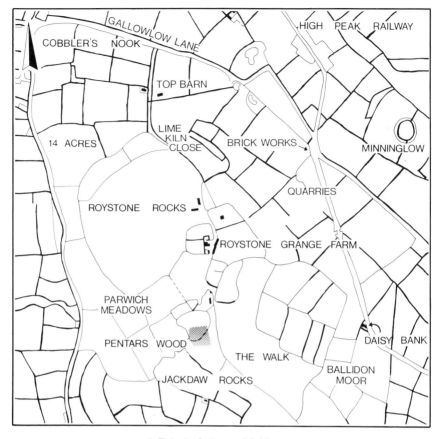

5. Principal sites and field names.

Few trees now grow in this landscape, though over the years small plantations have been installed to conceal old lead workings, or simply to shield the stock when the weather is at its most ferocious. Yet it is not a harsh landscape. The verdant, sometimes lush, growth of spring grass, speckled with moon daisies and other flowers, makes it stunningly beautiful on sunny days. The sweep of the fields and the spacious rolling vistas, even in a harsh winter light, create the spirit of the place.

We began the Roystone Grange Project in 1978 by making a survey of an area approximately 2 × 2 km which incorporates much of the present-day farm, and a little of what used to be known as Ballidon Moor, where the deserted farm of Daisy Bank is situated. Over the past ten years we have mapped over 70 kilometres of field walls, recorded all the earthworks, dug hundreds of pits across the pasture to find the buried traces of prehistoric man, and excavated a number of the larger settlements. All this has shown that the present farm is only the last in a long line. Indeed even the place-name, meaning 'reeve's stones' or 'raven's rocks' according to Professor Kenneth Cameron, belongs to the medieval Cistercian settlement here and so takes no account of the preceding four thousand years of farming.

Most people who visit the farm are surprised to learn that there has been a community here more or less continuously over the last six thousand years. Its isolation and, above all, the weather for much of the year defy the logic of twentieth-century living. There is no doubt that the weather is often harsh. Roystone is situated at about the same height above sea-level as the nearby weather-station at Buxton. Buxton has about 52 inches of rain a year, whereas Matlock, in a valley to the east of the White Peak, has only 31 inches. It is worth noting that places like Northampton and Oxford in the Midlands have only 26 inches.

Roystone also shares with Buxton weather-station about 38 days a year with snow on the ground, in contrast to 17 days at Oxford. But we have to interpret modern weather data with some caution. The climate is always changing, and in warm periods the Derbyshire Dome has many advantages. In the second millennium BC, for example, the age of Stonehenge, summer temperatures were probably 2-3°C higher than they are now. A similar optimum occurred between the tenth and twelfth centuries AD. Likewise there have been periods of climatic deterioration, such as early in the first millennium BC and between the thirteenth and seventeenth centuries (known as the Little Ice Age) which were times of high summer rainfall and long winters. Climate has an economic impact, because in present conditions oats and root crops can be grown at this altitude, but these would not prosper in wetter conditions. With heavy rainfall, although the hilltops drain well, the valleys do not. On the other hand, the thin soils require regular replenishment and can be easily over-grazed, even by rabbits, so turning a rich sward into a poor matted heathland. Summer heatwaves burn up the grass, but continual summer rain hinders the gathering of hay to feed the stock through the long winter months when the grass does not grow. The climatic equations are part of farming and well known to traditional farmers. In modern terminology, therefore, Roystone is a marginal farm.

Yet we must shake off all modern impressions when we begin to explore the history of Roystone Grange and similar farms in the White Peak. Today a global market in foodstuffs enables us to buy tropical and Mediterranean foods in any village shop in the Peak District and, for reasons defined by the EEC, farms like Roystone function in tune with the subsidies. In the past, however, Roystone operated within different economic spheres which, over six thousand years, have taken many forms. As we shall see, it was not always marginal. In some periods it figured in the mainstream of British and European

6. Looking south from Roystone over Ballidon quarry (photo: Ray Manley).

agriculture, and in others its pastures were not needed. Over the millennia the connections betwen the White Peak and the Trent Valley – as flint implements, Roman-period pottery, medieval building styles, and even the history of the railway show – were of fundamental importance to growth in both areas. The history of the uplands, in other words, tells us much about the so-called champion landscapes of central and southern England. This is because the rhythms of Peakland history are effectively accentuated versions of the champion lands. In some ways it might be said that the Peakland contains the high-water marks of those ages of expansion, which were clearly imprinted on the landscape whenever the growth in the economy receded. These high-water marks, we shall claim, are signposts for our understanding of the history of England.

The landscape

The landscape at Roystone is particularly striking. The farm itself lies half-way down a dry valley that provides a route from the White Peak plateau down to the rolling hills beyond Ballidon. The topography is rather more complex than this, however. The eastern side of the valley is made of carboniferous limestone which forms the principal structure of the Derbyshire Dome and after which the White Peak is named. This

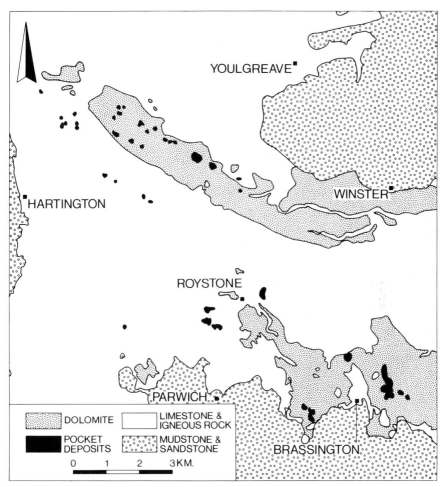

7. Outcrops of pocket sands in the southern part of the Derbyshire Dome (based on the British Geological Survey).

side of the valley contains particularly good stone for building. Indeed in the Edwardian period and throughout the First World War part of this hillside was quarried. Two kilometres south of the farm a quarry begun in 1945 has been enormously enlarged, and from the High Peak Trail (once the High Peak Railway) to the east of Roystone we can look down into this huge cavernous hole and see the monstrous machines which work there. The Geological Memoir for this region records that the limestone beds contain shelly fauna with *Gigantoproductus*, *Megachonetes siblyi* and *Palaeosmilia murchisoni*. The Roman and medieval builders at Roystone were evidently attracted by these fine fossiliferous slabs, while the stone proved excellent material in the Napoleonic period for enclosing the lands with a network of walls.

1. Interrogating the Landscape

The western side of the valley, however, takes a very different form. Roystone Rocks, for example, the hill behind the farm, is a rugged outcrop of crags and small tors that in some lights resembles Dartmoor. These outcrops are a form of carboniferous limestone which has been altered locally to dolomite. They occur quite commonly in the southern part of the Derbyshire Dome, and according to the Geological Memoir are probably the result of exposure to magnesian brines percolating from the Zechstein sea in late Permian times. The patchy distribution of the dolomite may reflect the extent to which the impermeable cover of Namurian mudstone was stripped from the region when the limestone was dolomitised.

Where the two rock-types meet in the valley bottom there are multi-coloured sands known as pocket deposits which have been trapped and preserved by collapse into solution cavities in the limestone and dolomite. The sands in these pockets range from deep reds to ochrous yellows and sometimes contain bands of chert. One deposit was exposed beside the old dairy, north of Roystone Grange Farm, and was studied during the project. The medieval grange is located on top of a second deposit. A third deposit at the north end of the farm was excavated by Victorian brick-makers, who took these silica sands to make refractory bricks in the yard beside the railway (see Chapter 6). Today the pit is partly flooded, but sections of banded pebbly clay can be seen, ranging in colour from red and purple to yellow, white and brown.

Few trees grace this landscape today. Pentars Wood is the only coppice in the valley; it lies behind the medieval grange, but its presence reminds us that the open pastures may belong to recent millennia. The wood contains a substantial rookery as well as a large badger set – an ecology, in other words, that is strikingly different from the world of larks, lapwings and moon daisies that typify most parts of the farm. How the topography of the landscape itself has altered over time remains an enigma. But it would be an error to believe that it has always been as it is today. Areas of woods and shrubs may well have covered the valley sides and even the tops. The absence of these today offers the walker magnificent panoramic views of the White Peak and the Midlands. It has also enabled the archaeologist to trace with ease the lumps and bumps left by past activities. Many of these are obvious, and they have been plundered by wall-builders and farmers over the centuries. Archaeologists too have long appreciated that this largely unploughed landscape makes it relatively easy to identify monuments.

The discovery of Roystone Grange

We were not the first archaeologists to discover Roystone. They have been visiting the area for two hundred years. The first recorded visit

8. Thomas Bateman, aged 38, and his son Thomas William, aged 8. Portrait by Thomas J. Banks, now in Sheffield City Museum (photo: Trevor Corns).

was by Dr Samuel Pegge and Major Hayman Rooke, who made a plan of Minninglow in May 1786 which was published in the Rev. James Douglas's *Nenia Britannica* (1793). Pegge and Rooke's investigations were modest by Victorian standards. Yet they may have excited the young William Bateman's fascination with the past when he moved

9. Cross-section of the Blackstone's Low cairn on Ballidon Moor, excavated in 1849, showing a crouched skeleton in a stone cist surmounted by a later cremation in a collared urn (from T. Bateman's *Ten Years' Diggings in Celtic and Saxon Grave-hills*, 1861).

with his father to Middleton-by-Youlgreave in 1815. Bateman soon began opening barrows in the vicinity of the family home and by 1826 had become a Fellow of the Society of Antiquaries of London. But the activities of William Bateman and his fellow antiquarians of the Peak have been overshadowed by the fame of his son, Thomas. William had married the nineteen-year-old Mary Compton from Rowsley in 1820, at which time he also became a partner in a paper mill with Mary's father. Thomas, who was born on 8 November 1821, was named after his grandfather. His mother lived only until the following July, leaving him to be brought up by his father and grandfather in Middleton Manor. When William died in 1835, aged only 47, young Thomas decided to continue with his father's hobby.

Thomas Bateman, in his short life, was to become one of the most distinguished English antiquarians. Beginning with an excavation at Bee Low in June 1843, he went on to open hundreds of barrows in Derbyshire and Staffordshire. The details of his excavations are ably recorded in his two books *Vestiges of the Antiquities of Derbyshire* (1848) and *Ten Years' Diggings in Celtic and Saxon Grave-hills in the counties of Derby, Stafford and York* (1861). He retraced Pegge and Rooke's steps to Minninglow, and in July 1843 set about an excavation. The burial mound, however, had probably been damaged in the intervening years by workmen seeking stone to build the enclosure walls on this high pasture (see Chapter 2). A week later he returned to open a cairn close to the railway. In this he found four skeletons, two of which were in a central cist made of limestone slabs.

Bateman seems subsequently to have ignored this corner of the Peak. But he steadily built up a reputation, and in September 1844 he attended the British Archaeological Association's conference at Canterbury to describe his investigations. He took with him his young mistress, Mary Ann Mason, and together they encountered the idiosyncratic Stephen Isaacson. Isaacson was a minor Byronic figure. Born in 1798, the son of an auctioneer, he had studied at Christ's College, Cambridge, where he began to write humorous verse, selling some of it to the *Gentleman's Magazine*. On graduating he took holy orders and in 1826 was adopted by the parish of St Paul's Demerara in the British West Indies, where he married Anna Miller of Barbados. He returned in 1832, a vehement opponent of slavery. By the 1840s he was evidently disliked for his views and was forced to take a poor parish at Dymchurch in Kent. There he fell in with the barrow-openers, and at the congress he was given the opportunity to deliver some of his doggerel to England's assembled antiquarians. Bateman clearly took to Isaacson and paid for him to visit Middleton for a month in 1845. Isaacson seems to have returned often that spring and summer, during which time he composed his long poem *Barrow-Digging by a Barrow-Knight*.

This poem, richly illustrated with lithographs by Llewellynn Jewitt, describes a typical day out:

> Uprouse ye then, my barrow-digging men,
> It is our opening day!
> And all exclaimed, their grog whilst swigging,
> There's naught on earth like barrow digging!

It recalls a day excavating a barrow near Wetton in the Staffordshire part of the White Peak. In one of the accompanying lithographs Bateman is busy with a pick and Isaacson, dressed in clerical garb, wields a trowel, while among the rest are Bateman's close associate Samuel Carrington and William Parker who worked on the Bateman estate. Bateman's greyhound, Nutt, also figures in the picture and poem.

> And barrow-knights are merrywights,
> When the find first greets their eye,
> For dagger or celt, or spear or belt,
> Wake all their sympathy.
> From morn till noon – or rising moon,
> They'll delve in ancient Lowe;
> And sing and laugh, and the rich wine quaff,
> When at home their spoils they show.

17

10. Vignette of William Parker, aged 29 (from Barry Marsden's *The Barrow Knight*, 1988).

11. Engraving by F.W. Lock showing the opening at Taylor's Low, Wetton, on 28 May 1845, described by Stephen Isaacson. *Left to right*: Isaacson, Benjamin Thompson, William Parker, David Swindell and Thomas Bateman (with pick). The gentleman in a top hat is probably a visitor. Bateman's dog, Nutt, is guarding the digging equipment in the foreground (from Barry Marsden's *The Barrow Knight*, 1988).

18

12. Small lead tablet stamped T. BATEMEN, placed by Thomas Bateman in the barrows that he excavated in imitation of Richard Colt Hoare (courtesy of Sheffield City Museum).

Isaacson evidently intended to emulate W.A. Miles's *The Deverel Barrow* (1826) and the Rev. C.S. Wooll's *The Barrow Diggers* (1839). Indeed, since each of the six Fyttes of the parson's poem is introduced with an elegiac description of the deep river gorges or the cross-country trips in a trap, he may even have had some of Byron's masterpieces in mind. The press, however, were not convinced, and the poem seems to have excited little interest after its publication in August 1845. By this time Bateman and Isaacson had fallen out. Bateman's biographer, Barry Marsden, speculates that the rift may have arisen because Isaacson drew attention to Bateman's adulterous liaison with Mary Ann Mason, who was the wife of a boatman at Cromford, and to his affair with the teenage Fanny Walton.

Bateman's passion for barrow-digging increased, and it wasn't long before he was back at Minninglow. On 18 July 1849 he made a cutting into the large cairn at Minninglow. Two days later he excavated a small barrow close by containing Romano-British finds. On the 27th he tackled the smaller barrow at Minninglow, finding that the earthen mound had been heaped up over (what he interpreted to be) the burnt remains of a funeral pyre. Early in August he moved westwards to explore barrows around Parwich. Then on 13 August he spent the day excavating at Ryestone Grange (as he called it). A recently built field wall bisected this barrow, preventing him from discovering the primary interment. He did, however, find an iron knife which he identified as Early Saxon (see Chapter 3). Two days later, on the 15th, he returned to the farm and tried in vain to find something in the largely destroyed mound close by the Roystone Grange barrow (see Chapter 3).

In 1849 Bateman had opened a total of 24 barrows and re-opened another five. Excessive though this may seem, it is worth noting that Dean Merewether, famous for his tunnel into Silbury Hill, actually dug

13. Thomas Bateman's museum at Lomberdale Hall from an 1851 lithograph (courtesy of Sheffield City Museum).

35 barrows between 18 July and 14 August. Bateman, however, was never to be quite so active again. In 1850 he was seriously ill and in the next year hardly ventured into the field, though he revisited Minninglow twice. In September he opened up the barrow beside the great cairn. A faint pen-and-ink drawing by his friend Brushfield shows a pick-man busy at work while a lady in a bonnet and a man in a top-hat observe the proceedings. Bateman made one further visit to this exposed spot on 10 November (when it is difficult to imagine that he kept his top-hat on). Thereafter his days out barrow-digging became fewer and fewer until his premature death in 1861, two months after publishing his second book.

Bateman's contribution to Peakland archaeology was enormous. Despite his rudimentary techniques – efficient though they were in one sense – we must be grateful to him for publishing two detailed books about his exploits. This rich documentation has helped archaeologists ever since to use his work as a starting-point for their different investigations into the past.

Samuel Carrington, Bateman's associate, continued to work in the Peak for several years after his mentor's death. His most ambitious project was to clear out Thor's cave near Wetton in 1864-65. Other associates, such as John Fossick Lucas of Fenny Bentley, continued

14. A workman stands outside Ravencliffe Cave, excavated by W. Storrs Fox between 1902 and 1906 (courtesy of Sheffield City Museum).

the Bateman style of barrow-opening. Among the barrows opened by Lucas is Wigber Low near Kniveton, the scene of John Collis's open-area excavations, which began in 1975 and are still continuing (they are described in Chapter 3). The fascination for barrow-digging, however, diminished after the 1860s, following *inter alia* the publication of Charles Darwin's *Origin of Species*. Darwin's great book, with its emphasis upon the evolution of mammalian life, refuted the

15. The late J.P. Heathcote in his museum at Birchover in 1979 (courtesy of Sheffield City Museum).

Renaissance idea, based in the chronology of the Bible, that the world had been created in 4004 BC. This spurred archaeologists to excavate settlement sites and eschew barrows. Settlement excavations, of course, had long taken place in classical archaeology, and even Samuel Carrington, under Bateman's supervision, had excavated a Romano-British village near Wetton. But by the turn of the century local archaeologists like W. Storrs Fox, headmaster of St Anselm's preparatory school, Bakewell, were much more interested in the riches to be found in clearing caves, such as at Harborough Rocks and Dimins Dale, than in sinking a shaft into a cairn.

Storrs Fox's excavations were primitive by the standards of the past eighty years. During this time the Peak District has benefited from the energetic activity of some fine archaeologists. Sir Ian Richmond, later professor of Roman archaeology at Oxford, carried out extensive excavations at the Roman fort at Brough in the Hope Valley. J.P. Heathcote of Birchover spent many years exploring Stanton Moor. In the 1960s Jeffrey Radley, an up-and-coming professional archaeologist, carried out many innovative excavations and surveys in the Peak. Tragically, he was killed in York when the side of his excavation trench fell in upon him. He encouraged many amateurs to carry out survey work, and from this period dates a remarkable study of

Romano-British villages in the Peak by Leslie Butcher, a surveyor with Sheffield City Council. In the past decade we have seen many changes in the management of archaeology in the region. The Trent & Peak Archaeological Trust, a team of professional archaeologists based in Nottingham, carry out major rescue excavations funded by the Department of the Environment through English Heritage. Furthermore the County Council and Peak Park Planning Board each employ a professional archaeologist to monitor the conservation, recording and presentation of archaeology in the area. Times have changed a good deal since Bateman went out barrow-digging. Indeed, if he were alive today, every effort would be made to stop him from indiscriminately plundering barrows. What took him a day to do now takes weeks, even months, and involves many people and a good deal of equipment. Often it may seem that the modern approach turns archaeology into the driest dust that blows (to paraphrase Sir Mortimer Wheeler). Yet, provided the right questions are asked, we believe that Bateman might have approved of modern efforts. In the case of Roystone Grange, at least, we have begun to make sense of the barrows he found, by considering them as part of the total history of a farming community.

The Roystone Grange Project

Archaeology is normally thought of as the study of single sites (such as Stonehenge) or of objects. Bateman certainly practised this sort of archaeology: he concentrated on burial mounds and their contents. But British archaeology in the twentieth century has become renowned for an altogether different approach. Its practitioners call it *landscape archaeology*, and it involves studying past landscapes and the communities within them in their totality. It includes mapping ancient fields, tracks and animal pens, as well as settlement sites and barrows, and tries to trace the remains of each phase of landscape use from modern times back to the earliest settlement. In some respects it resembles an excavation in which the past is brought to light layer by layer, often in a fragmented way. But landscape archaeology involves a good deal of surveying, aerial photography, study of vernacular architecture and, of course, carefully conceived excavations.

This peculiarly British form of archaeology owes its origins to several different sources. O.G.S. Crawford, a pioneer of aerial photography after the First World War, showed that many hitherto unknown monuments could be identified from the air. These ploughed-out monuments were no more than marks accentuated by the differential growth of crops, or by earthworks, barely discernible on the ground but clearly visible from the air when the angle of the sun created long shadows. At about the same time Sir Cyril Fox made an innovative study, *The Personality of Britain* (1932), which revealed the extraordinary richness of minor monuments that had survived the intensification of agriculture in Victorian times. Fox's perspective was presented even more eloquently in W.G. Hoskins's seminal *The Making of the English Landscape* (1955) which set out to show that an extraordinary range of monuments from prehistoric to modern times survived in the English countryside and might be used to write history as if they were documents. Hoskins asserted that

> behind the features of the landscape, behind tools or machinery, behind what appear to be the most formalised written documents, and behind institutions, which seem almost entirely detached from their founders, there are men, and it is men that history seeks to grasp. Failing that, it will be at best but an exercise in erudition. The good historian is like the giant of the fairy tale. He knows that wherever he catches the scent of human flesh, there his quarry lies.

Hoskins also declared with barely concealed passion that 'most academically-trained historians are completely blind to the existence and value of visual evidence. Visually speaking, they are still illiterate.' Hoskins's passion stemmed to some extent from his painful realisation that his sources were being destroyed faster than he could record them. Legions of scholars were needed to avoid the calamity that occurred when, subsidised by EEC grants, farmers introduced new machinery and extreme forms of agricultural intensification (notably the deep plough). In answer to his pleas, a small army of archaeologists in the late 1960s began to map the monuments of the endangered countryside. The Royal Commission for Historic Monuments led the way with fine surveys of Cambridgeshire, Dorset, Hampshire and Northamptonshire. At this time a major project was devised to record the threatened landscape archaeology of the Fens, and another examined the archaeology of Dartmoor. These large-scale investigations have produced extraordinary charts of landscapes in prehistoric, Romano-British and medieval times that echo, and in some cases virtually emulate, modern Ordnance Survey maps. On a smaller scale parish surveys, initiated in the 1960s, of Chalton, a chalkland village in Hampshire, and Wharram Percy in the Yorkshire Wolds have a basis in landscape archaeology but, through the medium of full-scale excavations, make it possible to record the history of a community in some detail over many millennia.

Until recently landscape archaeology has been a largely academic investigation, aimed at salvaging endangered historical sources. Recording and indeed conserving our heritage for posterity is undeniably an important responsibility of any generation. No one would now consider burning documents in the Public Record Office; likewise no one should ignore the evidence lying around our fields and hills, often unnoticed. In recent years, however, the social duties of the archaeologist have been strengthened by the realisation that the heritage industry is actually one of the largest economic enterprises in the country. More than 5 per cent of Britain's revenue comes from foreign currency brought in by tourists. Most of them come here not for our weather or our wine; it is our heritage that fascinates them. Britain's tourist managers, and indeed her archaeologists, have been slow to appreciate this. Visitors are directed too readily to honey-pots like Bath, Stonehenge or the innovative Jorvik Centre in York.

Yet in academic terms Britain has perhaps the best-mapped, best-presented heritage in the world, which should be made available to these huge numbers of visitors. The critical factor, of course, is to educate the lay visitor to benefit from such an interpretation of the past. This will not happen overnight. It has taken twenty-five years for ecologists and ornithologists to make the living planet an integral part of our own world. As a result, garden birds and flowers are now treated with as much respect and fascination as eagles or rare orchids.

This thought was clearly in our minds when we began at Roystone Grange. Since the farm lies in the Peak District National Park there was always the expectation that our investigations might be translated into 'visitor-friendly' results. The National Park, it should be remembered, is visited by an estimated 18½ million people each year, but although, as a recent report commissioned by the Park authorities concludes, most of them appreciate the fine landscapes, they are poorly informed about their remarkable heritage.

Hence the project began as a training exercise for first-year students from Sheffield in the hope that its results might benefit visitors who were interested in walking across a fine landscape and were mildly intrigued by its long history. Soon, as we understood the development of this landscape, in the manner first established by Crawford, Fox and Hoskins, we decided to link the discoveries by a trail. This trail has proved a great success; but it is only one facet in bringing archaeologists closer to the public to meet the historical needs of a generation which, with few exceptions, has little instinctive interest in six millennia of hill-farming.

2

Wall-to-Wall History

I wish you could have been there on the hill summit – the valley all white
... and just round us ... the grey stone fences drawn in a network over the
snow, all very clear in the sun.

D.H. Lawrence in a letter to
Katherine Mansfield, December 1918.

Many visitors to the Peak District are at once attracted and puzzled by
the endless miles of drystone walls that cover the valleys in a maze,
ascend the steep hills and disappear over the highest lows. The walls
add a vital ingredient to the landscape, casting deep shadow lines in
the sunshine and etching out hillsides on gloomy days. Walls, in fact,
seem a natural part of the landscape – a distinctive feature of the
Pennines, in contrast to the hedge country to the south.

Walls, of course, are not natural. Most of them were constructed in
the later eighteenth century after the passing of the Enclosure Acts
(see p. 131). Some, it was always assumed, belong to earlier periods.
Drystone walling was first used in the Peak District in Neolithic
chambered tombs. Tombs like Minninglow and Five Wells, near
Taddington, were built in the third millennium BC. The technique was
commonly employed to revet the edges of the many Bronze Age tombs
dotted about the Peak. The barrow at Wigber Low, for example,
recently excavated by John Collis, has a fine curb holding back the
cairn of stones. Several of the prehistoric barrows at Roystone appear
also to have curbs (see Chapter 3). The Bronze Age dwellings on Big
Moor (on the eastern flank of the National Park) were made of
drystone walling, roofed with thatch or turf, as were the defences of the
Iron Age hillfort at Carl Wark overlooking Hathersage. The art of
making walls was commonly practised in this region long before the
Romans.

It is one thing to identify walling within ancient settlements,
another to identify ancient field walls. Ancient field walls have been
found in many parts of upland Britain. On Dartmoor, for instance,
remains of a widespread network of walls, known as reaves, have been
attributed to the Bronze Age. Traces of similar walls have been found

associated with the prehistoric dwellings on the gritstone parts of the East Moors of the Peak District (see p. 68). In neither case are there modern walls of the enclosure period to complicate the archaeologist's task. Roystone, by contrast, is a landscape of walls.

To make sense of the problem at Roystone we began by examining all the different types of walling on the farm. It was soon clear that stretches of fossilised walling existed that were quite unlike the enclosure period walls. Equally, it was obvious that walls made in several different ways still stand to their full height. Of course it is possible that all these different types of wall are variations on the type constructed in the late eighteenth century. Sceptics are often tempted to lay greater emphasis on a simple explanation like this, being unable or unwilling to see how the well-documented episode of parliamentary enclosures is the most recent of many such episodes in the long history of the landscape. To counter this explanation it is necessary to demonstrate the relationship between each of the wall-types, as well as their association with ancient habitation sites. Invariably, since walls cannot be dated by carbon-14 to a precise year, sceptics will not be unduly impressed by the relationship between the wall-types; only evidence of the association of a wall-type to a habitation, usually as a result of excavation, makes an interpretation possible. Hence the typology of walls and their associated features presented in the following pages has been checked as far as possible by excavations. Doubtless some mistakes are made by this method; but, trusting in the eye of faith where scientific criteria have failed us, we hope that our interpretation encourages others to examine our hypotheses on the ground.

A typology of field walls

Type 1. Enclosure walls

Built as it is in straight, obviously surveyed, lengths, this type of wall generally ignores natural features in the landscape. In some places large dolomite boulders occur in the foundations at intervals of about a metre, presumably marking the lines laid out by the land-surveyors. For the most part, though, the foundations are indistinguishable from the body of the wall and are set in a shallow trench after the turf and topsoil have been removed. The fabric of the wall is made of small quarried carboniferous limestones of angular appearance. This type of wall is faced on both sides, its core being filled with small stones and chippings. Through-stones occasionally hold the two faces together. The top of the wall is finished with a row of transverse capping stones, set on edge in such a way as to bind the two sides together at the top. In cross-section this type has a battered appearance, being narrower at

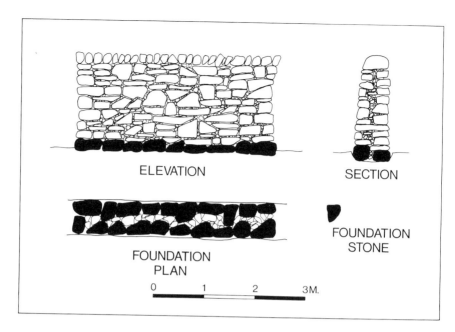

ELEVATION

SECTION

FOUNDATION
PLAN

FOUNDATION
STONE

0   1   2   3M.

16. Type 1 field wall.

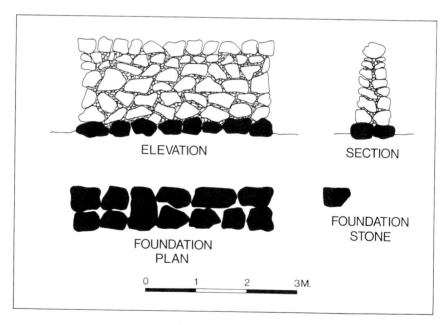

ELEVATION

SECTION

FOUNDATION
PLAN

FOUNDATION
STONE

0   1   2   3M.

17. Type 2 field wall.

28

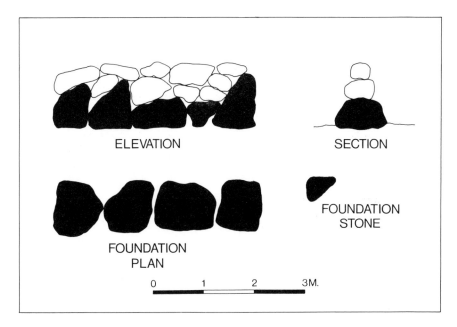

ELEVATION

SECTION

FOUNDATION
STONE

FOUNDATION
PLAN

0   1   2   3M.

18. Type 3 field wall.

the top than at the bottom. On average walls of this type tend to be about 150-180 cm high, 50-60 cm wide at the bottom and 40 cm wide at the top.

This type is difficult to date precisely, but it resembles the enclosure-period walls constructed around Parwich from 1788, for example, and at Brassington after an Act of Parliament of 1803. At Roystone it should date to about 1800.

Type 2. Post-medieval walls

Constructed in lengths that are almost straight but have a tendency to wander a metre or two in either direction, this type often respects or takes advantage of a natural feature in the landscape. The foundations consist of two rows of small dolomitic limestone boulders, laid firmly side-by-side, with every fourth or fifth boulder a through-stone. The foundations are set directly on the topsoil. Small, irregularly-shaped stones, almost certainly gathered from the surface, have been used to make the fabric of the wall. The body of the wall is made up of two faces with the voids left unfilled which narrow gradually to a top made of either small boulders or, less commonly, trimmed capping stones. As a rule walls of this type are 150-180 cm high, 60-80 cm wide at the bottom and 30-40 cm wide at the top.

This type is older than type 1 and younger than type 3 (see below). Walls of this type are associated with the enclosure of land on Ballidon

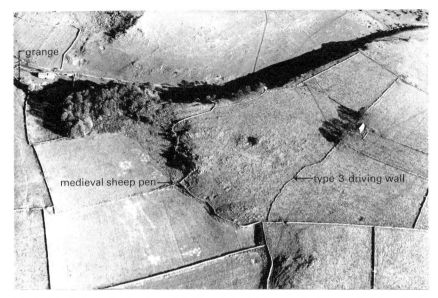

19. Aerial photograph of a type 3 field wall (a driving wall) close to Jackdaw Rocks (photo: Derrick Riley).

Moor – the land between Roystone and Ballidon Grange (later occupied by Daisy Bank Farm). Records of disputes between the two farms over the enclosing of this common land survive, dating to 1599 and 1612 (see p. 124). Similarly the will of Thomas Leving at Parwich, dated to 1639, contains details of his policy of enclosing land from common fields and shows that the disputes at Roystone were part of a pattern of such events occurring in this area in the early seventeenth century.

Type 3. Medieval walls

Only short lengths of this type remain standing to their full height. The foundations, however, are virtually indestructible, and long lengths continue to form the base of later walls. The foundations consist of massive dolomitic boulders which appear to have been heavily weathered, as though they had previously been dotted about the hillsides. The large stones are laid in a single row, directly on the topsoil. In the few instances where the entire wall survives it is clear that the foundations form the greater part. The upper fabric, as a rule, consists of one thickness of rough dolomitic stones which tend today to be pleasingly coated in lichens. The large gaps in the body of the wall (between the irregularly shaped boulders) make the wall appear unstable, which seems to deter sheep from trying to scramble over it. Walls of this type are about 100-120 cm high, 80-100 cm wide at the bottom and 20-30 cm wide at the top.

This type is overlain by type 2 and type 1 in many places, showing

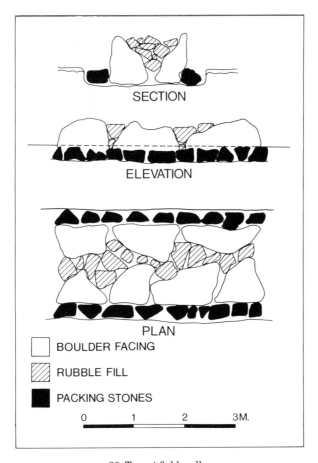

SECTION

ELEVATION

PLAN

☐ BOULDER FACING

▨ RUBBLE FILL

■ PACKING STONES

0   1   2   3M.

20. Type 4 field wall.

stratigraphically that it pre-dates the post-medieval period. A wall of this type is associated with a thirteenth/fourteenth-century phase of the Cistercian grange, and indeed its distinctive fabric resembles the earliest construction of the grange (see p. 101). We believe therefore that Garendon Abbey, the Cistercian monastery that acquired Roystone in the later twelfth century, was responsible for constructing the walls of this type.

Type 4. Romano-British walls

This distinctive type survives nowhere above foundation level. It consists of dolomitic or carboniferous limestone slabs set on edge in two parallel lines forming what is locally called a double-orthostat wall. The space between the two orthostats is filled with small boulders and rubble. Excavations show that the foundations were set into a shallow

31

21. Excavation of a type 4 field wall (photo: Richard Hodges).

22. A type 4 wall, originally constructed in the Romano-British period, winds its way up through the valley beyond Roystone Grange Farm (photo: Ray Manley).

trench, which was packed with small stones. There may be two phases of this type: an earlier phase distinguished by orthostats that have been split apart, and therefore have a regular appearance, and a later phase when irregularly shaped boulders have been collected for this purpose. As a rule the foundations stand about 50 cm above the modern ground level and vary from 1-2 metres in width.

This type is dated by association with the Romano-British village at Roystone. Such a wall enclosed the farmyard for the largest dwelling in the village (p. 76). Similarly the outlying farm, known as Roystone Grange 2, lies within a larger enclosure wall of this type. Parallels are well-known in the Peak. At the Romano-British village of Rainster Rocks, 4 kilometres away, several dwellings are associated with paddocks made with double-orthostat walls. Further north, at Chee Tor above the Wye valley, where dolomitic limestone does not exist, the inhabitants of the large Romano-British village used carboniferous slabs to create the same effect. Similar walls were constructed on Carsington Pastures, about 7 kilometres east of Roystone, to divide up parcels of land rich in lead. In sum, for reasons which will be described in Chapter 4, the double-orthostat wall seems to have been introduced to the White Peak during the second century AD.

Type 5. Prehistoric walls

Found only in one area of Roystone, on the hill known as Roystone Rocks, walls of this kind were used to make a small enclosure. The remains consist of long, carefully selected boulders laid end to end on the topsoil. No trace of the body of the wall has survived. The foundations are one stone's thickness, varying from 10-20 cm, and from 40-50 cm wide.

Two excavations were made through this enclosure wall in an attempt to date it. One of these cuttings produced potsherds of Early Bronze Age date. Two larger excavations on the platform within the enclosure brought to light a range of worked flint and chert of from Mesolithic to Bronze Age date, but no more recent material. For reasons which will be described in Chapter 3, we propose an Early Bronze Age date for this type. A possible parallel for this enclosure exists in front of the rock-shelter excavated by Jeffrey Radley at Sheldon on the White Peak plateau. Here, much as on Roystone Rocks, a wall closes off an early prehistoric site where traces of Bronze Age activity occur. Other walled enclosures of the period have recently been identified on Big Moor in the northern part of the Peak.

Banks, gates, stiles and sheep-creeps

Besides the walls other features of the ancient farming landscape have

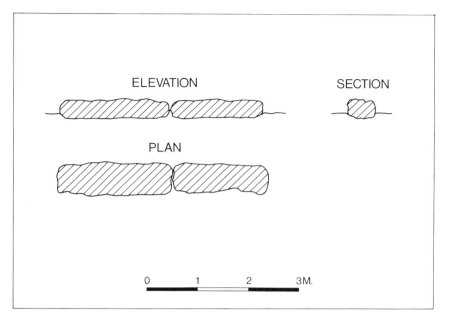

ELEVATION   SECTION

PLAN

0   1   2   3M.

23. Type 5 field wall.

been preserved at Roystone. There are field banks which once divided up plots of worked ground. Gateposts survive, incorporated as often as not in later walls or, like old molars, pulled out and left by the gateway. Stiles too survive from periods long before the age of leisure. Often these indicate the lines of ancient routeways across the landscape. Finally there are sheep-creeps to allow sheep to squeeze through a wall into another pasture. As in the case of the walls, by attempting to age these features we can throw new light on the use made of the farm at different stages in its history.

Banks

Two types of banks have been identified at Roystone, both of Romano-British date. Earthen banks varying from 1½ to 3 metres in width and surviving to a height of 20-30 cm occur in one field, respecting a Romano-British wall and overlain by a (later) medieval one. The profile of these banks may have been accentuated by medieval ridge-and-furrow agriculture in this field; indeed these banks may be the fossilised remains of Romano-British ploughing. By contrast the narrower earth and rubble banks on the steep slope known as the Walk were intended to divide up the small plots of land. These banks are about 1-2 metres wide and stand 20-30 cm high. Three cuttings through these banks produced several sherds of Romano-British pottery which may have arrived in these unlikely spots when they

34

24. Aerial photograph of Romano-British field banks (*centre*) surviving on a steep hillside (known as the Walk) in the southern enclosure at Roystone. It is likely that the entire enclosure was parcelled up in this way (photo: Derrick Riley).

were thrown onto the fields among farmyard manure. Ploughing or water action probably brought them to the edge of the field, and with time they became buried. The rubble in the bank probably comes from field clearance, around which soil has accumulated. Whether hedges grew on top of the banks remains a matter for speculation.

Gates

Five kinds of ancient gatepost survive at Roystone, as well as modern concrete, wooden and steel posts. These five types are:

(1) Natural dolomitic boulders
(2) Shaped dolomitic boulders
(3) Natural carboniferous slabs
(4) Dressed carboniferous posts
(5) Dressed gritstone posts

We have attempted to date the gateposts at Roystone using a combination of the material used and widths of gateways. Four widths of gateway occur:

35

(1) 3 feet (about 1 metre)
(2) 7 feet (about 2.10 metres)
(3) 10 feet (about 3 metres)
(4) 12 feet (about 3.60 metres)

Over the years, of course, many gates on the farm have been replaced and the gateways have been widened. Nevertheless enough survives in the ancient walls to make it possible to interpret the gates themselves. The basic types are:

(1) An original gateway where the wall on either side of the opening is of one build right up to the back of the gateposts and no traces exist of widening or a later insertion.

(2) A widened gateway where the original wall build runs up to the gatepost on one side, while the corresponding inserted gatepost has a length of infill walling beside it. Often a pile of stone can be found close by; and sometimes the original post will have been left nearby as well. Occasionally the wall foundations are left and can be seen in the widened gateway.

(3) An inserted gateway where piles of wall stone will be found on each side of the opening and the tell-tale infilling of the wall can be seen beside the posts.

Using all the information we conclude that:

(1) Natural dolomitic boulders are used as gateposts only in the type 3 (medieval) walls, with gateways that are either 1 metre or 2.10 metres wide. This appears to be a medieval gatepost.

(2) Shaped dolomitic boulder gateposts occur in wall types 1, 2 and 3. We believe that in the enclosure-period walls (type 1) they are original if the gateway is 3 metres wide, and represent widening of earlier walls if the gateway is 3.60 metres across. But if this gatepost occurs in type 2 walls (post-medieval) they are part of the original wall if the gateway measures 2.10 metres across and insertions if the gateway is either approximately 3 or 3.60 metres wide. Finally this gatepost only occurs in widened, that is later, insertions, in wall type 3. In sum this kind of gatepost was introduced in early post-medieval times.

(3) Natural carboniferous slabs are used as gateposts in wall types 1, 2 and 3. In type 1 they are original if the gateway is 3 metres wide, or an insertion if it is about 3.60 metres wide. In type 2 walls they are replacements if the gateway is 3 metres wide and later insertions if the gateway is of the two wider variations. When this kind of post occurs in the type 3 medieval walls it is always a later insertion. This gatepost type was probably introduced in the late eighteenth century.

(4) Dressed carboniferous posts occur in wall types 1, 2 and 3 and

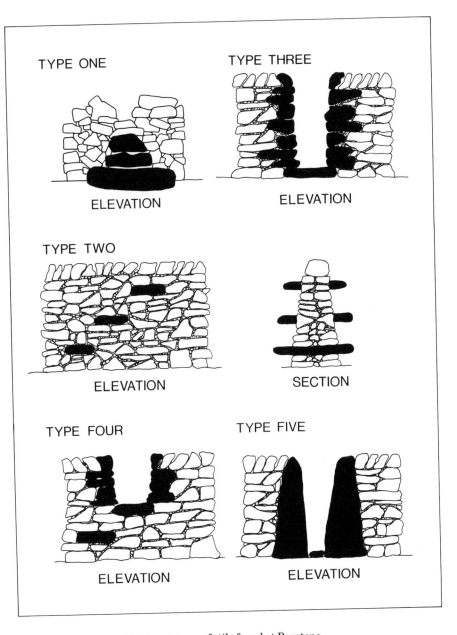

25. Different types of stile found at Roystone.

26. Type 5 stile (photo: Richard Hodges).

follow the same pattern as the natural carboniferous slabs.

(5) Dressed gritstone posts occur in wall types 1, 2 and 3 and belong to the same pattern as the natural carboniferous slabs. It is likely, though, that this type belongs to the second half of the nineteenth century, when the stone could be delivered by the High Peak Railway (see p. 144).

Stiles

Five kinds of stile are found at Roystone. Type 1 occurs beside the ruins of the small post-medieval dairy near the site of the medieval grange (see p. 127) and consists of three steps abutting the outside of the wall and leading up to a narrow gap. This is almost certainly a post-medieval stile. Type 2, where two or three long stones protrude beyond both faces of the wall, providing graded steps either side of the wall, may also belong to the post-medieval period. The following three

27. Type 2 sheep-creep through a type 2 wall (photo: Martin Wildgoose).

types, however, belong to the enclosure period: type 3 – a gap left in the body of the wall; type 4 – a combination of types 2 and 3 with two protruding steps leading to a gap in the wall; and type 5 – where a stone post stands each side of a gap in the wall.

Stiles, it seems, were not necessary before the enclosures of the seventeenth century. Even then they were few in number until the late eighteenth-century Enclosure Acts blocked off long-established rights of way.

Sheep-creeps

Sheep-creeps allow sheep to pass through small gaps in the wall. Two sorts occur at Roystone.

The first occurs in type 1 (enclosure-period) walls and has been inserted at a later date into wall types 2 and 3. Generally the opening is twice as high as it is wide. The jambs of the opening are usually made of more regular stones than the wall in which it is located. Often alternating courses have longer stones tying back into the fabric of the wall to give it more stability. A large carboniferous slab forms a lintel carrying the main body of the wall overhead.

A second type of sheep-creep occurs only in wall types 2 and 3 and appears to be medieval in origin. The opening is as high as it is wide with jambs consisting of single dolomitic limestone boulders. A long dolomitic boulder serves as a lintel carrying the body of the wall.

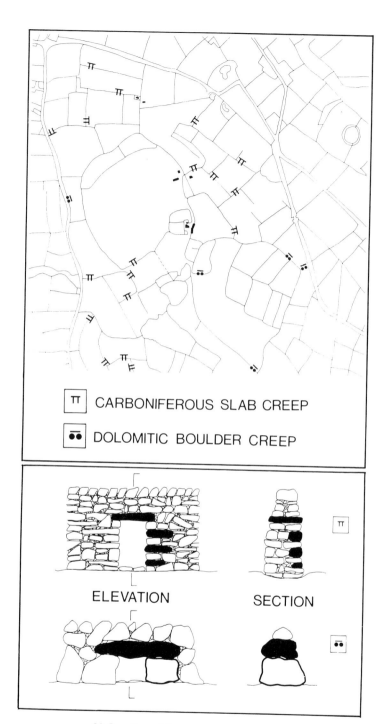

CARBONIFEROUS SLAB CREEP

DOLOMITIC BOULDER CREEP

ELEVATION   SECTION

28. Location of sheep-creeps at Roystone.

A farm through the ages

In the following chapters we shall describe each stage in the history of Roystone Grange. At this point it may be helpful to give general guidance to the reader using the combination of evidence found from our study of the walls and allied features.

Fig. 29 shows all the type 1 enclosure-period walls. Few of the walls in the heart of the farm were constructed in this period. Instead type 1 walls occur around the flanks of the valley and on the tops, forming a patchwork of new fields. Only the High Peak Railway cuts across this patchwork, showing that it was constructed after the ground was enclosed. The surviving lengths of type 2 walls (Fig. 30) form an entirely different pattern. These walls are few in number and for the most part sub-divide larger, pre-existing fields around the outer edge of the heart of the farm. Fig. 31, depicting the surviving remains of type 3 medieval walls, helps to explain the pattern of type 2 post-medieval walls. The map shows that these boulder walls were used to create a bounded estate as well as fields on either side of the farm itself. The type 2 post-medieval walls, in other words, were employed to sub-divide pre-existing medieval fields. But, like the type 2 walls, those of the medieval period were influenced by the preceding pattern

29. Type 1 walls at Roystone.

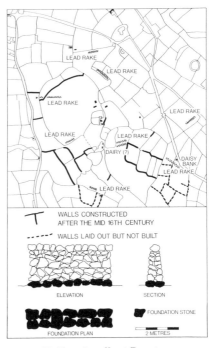

30. Type 2 walls at Roystone.

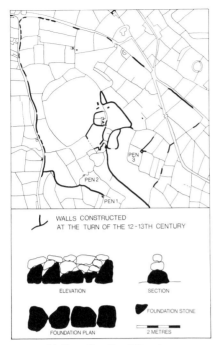

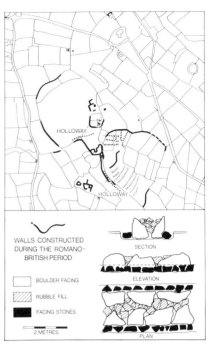

31. Type 3 walls at Roystone.

32. Type 4 walls at Roystone.

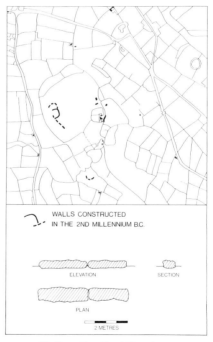

33. Type 5 walls at Roystone.

42

of walls – those of the Romano-British period. The type 4 Romano-British walls (Fig. 32) enclose two hills and, on paper at least, look like two wings of a butterfly on either side of the valley. The western wing encloses Roystone Rocks, a dolomitised carboniferous limestone hill. The eastern wing, parcelled up by linear banks into fields, contains a fine stretch of carboniferous limestone. The walls enclosing both wings follow natural features and, unlike all the later walls (types 1, 2 & 3), take no account of any pre-existing man-made additions to the landscape. The reason for this is clear when we turn to Fig. 33. The type 5 walls bear witness to a largely unenclosed landscape in prehistory.

The typology of walls permits us to strip off – layer by layer – the succession of changes made to Roystone over the past six millennia. By plotting the gates, tracks, stiles and sheep-creeps too we can begin to build up a picture of how the modern landscape has been shaped. Walls were employed in different ways at different stages in the history of Roystone. To understand these stages we have investigated the archaeology of the succession of farming communities themselves. Their farms, yards, pens and even their rubbish enable us to put flesh upon the skeletal picture formed by mapping the walls. With this mixture of information we can begin to reconstruct the history of the farm and its place in the making of the White Peak.

3

Four Thousand Years of Prehistoric Farming

It can only be said that centuries, perhaps tens of centuries, before the lust of conquest tempted the Roman Legions across the Channel – at a period, it may be, coeval with that in which the Egyptians toiled to accumulate those imperishable stone barrows, the Pyramids, while Abraham yet assembled his herds on the Mesopotamian pastures; and the cities of the Plain (soon to be overthrown), were yet accessible to the traveller; there existed in Britain a population, possibly pre-Celtic, at all events having habits corresponding with those which were universally disseminated by the primitive races in their radiations from the trans-Himalayan cradle of the species.

Thomas Bateman, *Ten Years' Diggings in Celtic and Saxon Grave-hills* (1861)

The cosy familiarity of a rolling landscape broken up by walls and copses makes it difficult to imagine what it was like in prehistory. The valleys were almost certainly far more wooded than they are today, and man's imprint upon the region was less marked. Reconstructing this lost world presents quite a challenge, calling us to shed familiar images and let the archaeology fire our imaginations instead. This is easier said than done. When we began at Roystone we were following in Bateman's footsteps as far as the prehistory of the region was concerned. There was no simple way to uncover the way of life of the prehistoric farming community. Indeed some prehistorians were convinced that the Derbyshire Dome was used only by seasonal pastoralists until the Romans arrived. Of course, we did not believe that the pre-Roman peoples of this region were descended from migrants that had originated in the Himalayas. Nevertheless, the starting-points for our investigation of the prehistoric landscape at Roystone were the sites that Bateman and his little band of associates had created as a result of their barrow-diggings.

Using the results of twentieth-century studies of prehistoric chronology, Peakland sites can now be ordered in a way that would have fascinated Bateman. There are cave sites, such as Thor's Cave in

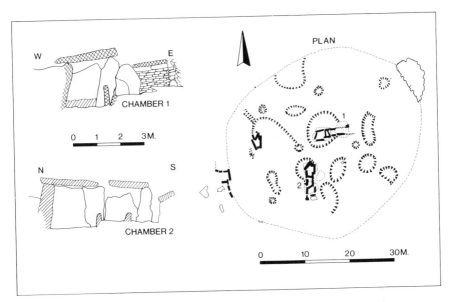

34. Minninglow: a plan and sections through two of the better-preserved megalithic chambers.

the Manifold Valley excavated by Samuel Carrington, which were probably first occupied about 15,000-10,000 BC, in what archaeologists term the Upper Palaeolithic period. Then there are many sites of the so-called Mesolithic period, dating from about 8000-4000 BC, when the hunter-gatherers developed a much finer technology. Bateman was not well-informed about this phase, which has come clearly into focus only since 1945. Notable among Mesolithic sites are Pin Hole Cave excavated by Don Bramwell, and the rock-shelter above Sheldon excavated by Jeffrey Radley. By contrast Bateman was fascinated by the Neolithic and Bronze Age cultures of the White Peak. He excavated Neolithic long barrows such as Green Low, Minninglow and Taddington and exposed their megalithic funerary chambers. We now know that these grand monuments, perhaps the first great man-made structures in the region, date to the third millennium BC, when the hunter-gatherer population started to practise horticulture and pastoralism. Next in the sequence are the great ritual sites at Arbor Low – the Stonehenge of the North, as it has been called – and the Bull Ring near Buxton. Like Stonehenge, these were probably constructed around 2000 BC, as the tribesmen of Britain looked increasingly to the science of astronomy to guide their agricultural practices. Evidently these henges were akin to cathedrals in the landscape, serving large populations who also erected stone circles such as those on Hart Hill Moor and Stanton Moor. At this time too the numerous round barrows and cairns, commonly situated near the henges and circles, were made. These simple monuments captivated Bateman, perhaps because in

45

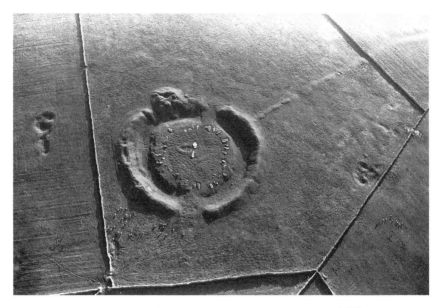

35. Aerial photograph of the henge at Arbor Low (photo: Derrick Riley).

common with other antiquarians at this time he saw them as Britain's answer to the pyramids.

Bateman had little interest in settlement sites, so prehistoric hillforts like Mam Tor overlooking the Hope Valley or Fin Cop above Monsal Dale escaped his spade. Indeed, because in his time British prehistory was compressed into a historical chronology formulated by students of ancient Egypt, Greece and Mesopotamia, Bateman probably assumed that the builders of Arbor Low and the deceased encountered in his many barrow-openings were members of the woad-painted primitive tribes found by Julius Caesar when he invaded Britain in 55 BC.

Bateman's perspective of the prehistory of the White Peak was consistent with the ethos of the Victorian Age. It was a past formed by sites and the objects they contained. In some ways it resembled a history of Britain composed of nothing but kings, queens and dates. This kind of history may hold few attractions today, but Bateman and his contemporaries were pioneers in search of a conceptual framework – the equivalents of kings and queens – for prehistory. Bateman's achievement was that his interpretation – in outline at least – prevailed until recently, indeed until long after the introduction of techniques such as radiocarbon dating.

When we began our work at Roystone in 1978 it was clear that British prehistory was at last shaking off the influence of the Victorian antiquarians. In recent times a strong interest in reconstructing the social and economic circumstances before the Roman Conquest has

46

36. H. St. George Gray's excavations of the henge bank at Arbor Low in 1903 (courtesy of Sheffield City Museum).

superseded their fascination with sites and objects. Using anthropological frameworks archaeologists have begun to re-examine many long-held axioms of British prehistory, such as the rigid division of the past into ages based upon their principal technological attributes. Similarly, the migrations of the so-called Beaker Folk or Iron Age tribesmen have been shown to be mistaken interpretations of the rather complex relations between the myriad tribes of western Europe in the second and first millennia BC. In recent years too archaeologists have begun to map the fields and enclosures that make up the prehistoric landscape. These maps show that a remarkable degree of order existed in the British countryside long before the Romans arrived. The most outstanding achievements in this area of research have been in uplands like Dartmoor and the North York Moors, where in the second millennium BC miles of fields were systematically laid out. These remarkable discoveries show that Britain in the age of Stonehenge was a densely populated and highly organised country. Now, as prehistorians apply ever-finer methods of interpretation to their data, a prehistory of Britain is being formulated in terms of evolving tribes and territories, modelled upon the documented tribal history of Anglo-Saxon England.

On one matter everyone is clear: the hunters, horticulturalists,

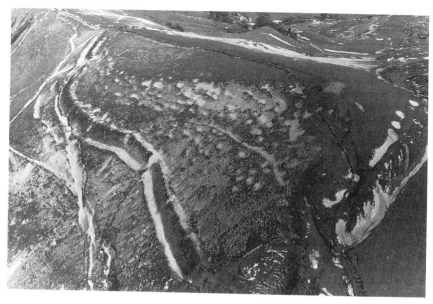

37. Aerial photograph of Mam Tor hillfort under snow (photo: Derrick Riley).

henge-builders and warriors of pre-Roman Britain evolved methods of managing the landscape that were in no sense primitive. The absence of pyramids and the like may challenge our picture of how civilisation should appear, but we are now beginning to understand how other communities in other times organised their world. At Roystone, the absence of early field walls challenged our picture of how a farm should look. Nevertheless we soon realised that the landscape held clues to its long prehistoric use other than in the form of the barrows that Bateman had found.

Barrow-diggers at Roystone

As we have seen, Isaacson's poem *Barrow-Digging by a Barrow Knight* provides a witty description of a barrow-opening expedition. Bateman and three or four others with his dog Nutt would set out early in a trap and head for the chosen mound. Bateman's books, in which each investigation is logged, show that he had an uncanny ability to select mounds containing antiquities. The trap carried the excavation equipment, as Isaacson records:

...bring the barrow tools,
Pick, shovel, scratcher, trowel, rules

and once at the mound it seems that a shaft little more than a metre by a metre was excavated using a pick and shovel for the early stages. Then, as Isaacson tells us,

Hither bring my trusty scratcher,
'Mongst barrow-tools there's none to match her,
And tread not heavily, because it
May seriously affect deposit,
For Briton's skull so long in ground
Is very seldom perfect found;
And what we scarcely deem a less ill
You may destroy a potter's vessel,
Which formed of potter's clay, though thick,
Can scarce withstand the blow of pick!

When Bateman first visited Ryestone Grange (as he called it) on 13 August 1849 he opened what we call Roystone Grange barrow 1

which is tolerably perfect ... 11 yards across and near four feet high, but crossed by a thick stone wall which greatly impeded our operations, and which there is reason to believe prevented the discovery of the primary interment. At one side of the wall we found many bones, both human and animal; the only undisturbed skeleton being that of a child, buried about a foot from the surface, and unaccompanied by anything of interest; among the animal bones were some teeth of dogs. On the other side of the wall we found an iron knife, of the usual Saxon shape, about a foot beneath the turf; and on the natural surface below, a deposit of calcined bones containing a bone pin. By undercutting the wall as far as practicable, we ascertained that the centre of the barrow was principally of earth surrounded by large stones inclining inwards, and from this locality we drew out a piece of curiously ornamented pottery of primitive manufacture.

This was the first of Bateman's two barrow-opening expeditions at Roystone. His second visit two days later was unsuccessful because wall-builders had destroyed the mound he intended to excavate. It is interesting to note that he overlooked at least another six barrows scattered in the immediate vicinity.

Roystone Grange barrow 1, however, is today an interesting monument. Its once prominent position has been destroyed by a First World War quarry that cut away much of its western side. Hence it now stands half-sectioned below the field wall that impeded Bateman, and it is easy to make out how the secondary barrow was constructed over a primary one. Bateman misled his readers, however, because it is evident that he dismantled a section of the type 1 enclosure-period wall to sink his shaft into the secondary mound. Here he found the knife and other Anglo-Saxon remains. But removing the wall must have slowed up his investigation, and the primary interment in the lower mound with its Bronze Age cist containing cremated bone and a flint plano-convex knife remained unexposed until cows rubbed against the section in July 1986. Here too we found a pair of iron tweezers which Bateman must have used, although Isaacson does not mention them in

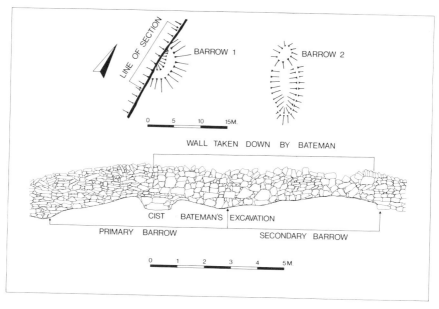

38. Section through Roystone Grange barrow 1 showing the primary barrow of prehistoric date and the Anglo-Saxon secondary barrow. The barrow has been half-removed by quarrying; another barrow (no. 2) lies close by.

39. Roystone Grange barrow surmounted by a type 1 field wall; Minninglow is in the background (photo: Richard Hodges).

50

his poem. One day, perhaps, if this barrow is exhaustively excavated, Bateman's lead calling card, planted on that August day, may be retrieved:

> A leaden label we enclose
> In pity to such late man,
> Where one and all may read, who choose,
> Inscribed the name, 'T. Bateman'.

In fact all the known tablets are stamped 'T. Batemen', a spelling error that did not unduly disturb the antiquarian (see Fig. 12).

Barry Marsden, Bateman's biographer, found a lead tablet during his excavations of Minninglow – the great Neolithic megalithic chambered tomb which crowns the hill on the eastern side of Roystone. The tablet lay within the debris filling chamber 4, where it was probably left after Bateman's campaign in 1851 (see Chapter 1). Between 1975 and 1976 Marsden also investigated a prominent barrow overlooking Roystone Grange Farm, which he at first believed was that excavated by Bateman in 1849. In fact this barrow (we have named it after the lime kiln cut into its west face) was missed by Bateman. Marsden's excavations were limited to a cross-shaped trench over the top of the barrow. Even so, he found the bones of a young person in a cist situated a little off the centre of the mound. The bones had been disturbed by a later insertion of a cremation urn (a Collared Urn type) associated with which were three flints, including two plano-convex knives like the one found in Roystone Grange barrow 1. South of the cist the disarticulated remains of two people were found associated with a Handled Food Vessel and a shattered Collared Urn. Nearby were three skulls, prompting the excavator to speculate about a Bronze Age head cult, or even cannibalism. A final, unurned cremation was discovered in the west side of the mound, and a later extended skeleton, probably accompanied by two Romano-British pins, was found on the south side. This small excavation reveals how packed with ancient remains these Peakland barrows are.

If this or any of the other barrows in the Roystone Grange cemetery were to be completely excavated using the techniques currently employed by John Collis at nearby Wigber Low, a different picture would almost certainly emerge. Wigber Low, a barrow first explored by John Fossick Lucas in Victorian times, has been entirely excavated, much as if it were a building rather than a mound containing pockets of treasure. A palimpsest of hilltop activities has come to light. The sequence is as follows. Dead bodies were evidently laid out on a platform here in the third millennium BC; then a Bronze Age cairn, neatly retained by a fine curb, was built on the spot, containing cremations like that found in the Roystone Grange barrow. Wigber

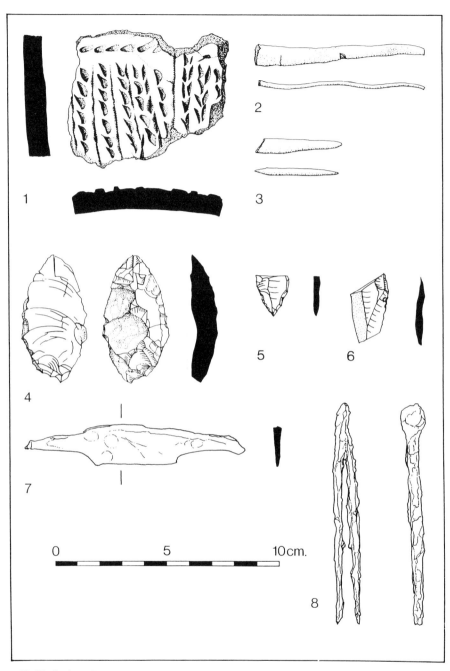

40. Finds from Roystone Grange barrow 1. 1: fragment of a Bronze Age urn decorated with finger-nail ornamentation; 2 & 3: worked bone; 4: a plano-convex flint knife; 5 & 6: worked flint implements; 7: the Anglo-Saxon knife described by Bateman; 8: Bateman's tweezers (?).

attracted Iron Age and Roman visitors who left their debris. In the seventh century AD an Anglo-Saxon household was interred in the barrow over two or three generations, and an associated secondary barrow was made. In the Middle Ages the barrow was used as a beacon and as a lead-smelting site. Later, like the smaller barrow at Roystone, it attracted the attention of eigtheenth-century wall-builders.

Uncovering Wigber Low has taken many months. Every stone is plotted, and the many thousands of bones and objects found have been recorded in three dimensions. As a result, using computer graphics, it is possible to reconstruct the barrow as it evolved stage by stage, and to locate the graves, finds and even the burrowing moles and shrews within this picture. Instead of inserting a lead tablet, and in keeping with the spirit of our times, John Collis rebuilt the mound, recreating an impression of Wigber as it would have looked in antiquity.

Monuments to the dead, however, like parish churches and their graveyards, only reveal a certain amount about the past. Many questions remain unanswered. Who founded the prehistoric barrow cemetery at Roystone Grange? When? How did they live? What happened after the cemetery was abandoned? What did the farm look like? These questions can only be answered by looking beyond the mounds and the antiquities they contain.

Prehistoric settlements in the Peak District have proved very elusive. Indeed some scholars believed that there were none to be found. Instead, they argued, the barrows were constructed by shepherds who brought their flocks up to the high ground in the warmer summer months. During this period, so the theory goes, they lived in tents and flimsy structures which have left no archaeological traces.

In one sense, however, archaeological traces of settlements do exist. In the 1960s, with the introduction of deep ploughing of selected high pastures, concentrations of flint implements and the debris from working and reshaping them were found. Jeffrey Radley plotted a scatter of this kind near Elton, two miles east of Minninglow. Another scatter was discovered a few years later on the slopes of Minninglow. In recent times similar scatters have been plotted all over the White Peak; large excavations of them were made at Aleck Low in 1979 and at Mount Pleasant near Kenslow in 1982. Almost no archaeological features were discovered at Mount Pleasant, while at Aleck Low traces of ard-marks and sunken features, possibly parts of dwellings, were found. In neither case, however, was it clear whether or not there had been some permanent habitation on these highly exposed spots.

This fascinating question provided us with the opportunity to explore the problem at Roystone. Was the barrow cemetery associated with farms or even a village, or was it where shepherds from the Trent Valley buried their dead in the summer?

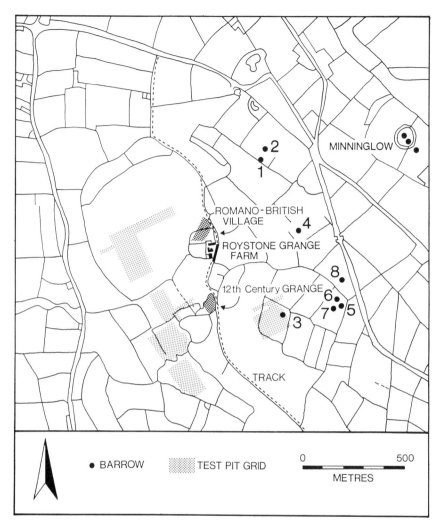

41. The Bronze Age barrow cemetery (barrows 1-8) and the extent of test-pitting at Roystone Grange. The areas test-pitted were Roystone Rocks, Parwich Meadows, Jackdaw Rocks and around the Lime Kiln barrow (3).

Test-pitting at Roystone

Few fields at Roystone have been ploughed in recent years. One field beside the Parwich track, however, was regularly planted with potatoes in the 1950s and 60s. During those years Mr D. Vallance, a railwayman working on the High Peak Railway, used to come down from the track and look among the furrows for flints. Here he found the

54

tiny, skilfully-worked Mesolithic flints known as microliths as well as Neolithic arrowheads and scrapers. Nowadays no field is ploughed on the farm and we therefore surmised that any prehistoric concentrations of debris would be situated more or less where they fell thousands of years ago. No single trench, however, was going to help us find these elusive buried lenses of prehistoric rubbish. Robin Torrence, a lecturer in archaeology at Sheffield University, offered to find a solution. She looked to America, where in the north-eastern woodland states a technique called shovel-testing is commonly used to locate otherwise undetectable sites. We modified the American methodology and gave it our own name – test-pitting. Essentially, this involved laying out a grid of squares across the landscape and excavating test-pits at regular intervals within this grid. The test-pits were spaced at 10-metre intervals, and each pit measured 0.5 × 1 metre. The pits were excavated stratigraphically, each apparent layer and associated finds being carefully recorded. Soil samples were taken, a measured drawing was made of the profile of the pit, and then the pit was back-filled. Back in the university, each category of find was recorded on computer, enabling us to compile maps showing their spread across the landscape. Our aim was to sample a significant part of Roystone by excavating hundreds of pits in an attempt to build up a picture of the concentrations of prehistoric debris.

A great deal of prehistoric material was found using this technique, as well as Romano-British, medieval and modern rubbish which also helps us to document what has become known as 'off-site' archaeology – manuring, work in the fields and even wall-building. In all, four large areas were pitted (Fig. 41):

(1) Roystone Rocks, on which the prehistoric (type 5) walled enclosure is located (see below, p. 57).

(2) Parwich Meadows bisected by the Parwich track, leading up to the Quarry Hill on the south side, and down to the Grange.

(3) Jackdaw Rocks, where the Romano-British farm Roystone Grange 2 is located.

(4) The hilltop above the Walk on which the Lime Kiln barrow (no. 3 on Fig. 41) is situated.

In all nearly 1,000 pits were excavated, involving the sweat and dedication of many students. Conscious of how labour-intensive this operation is, we selected each test area with care. On the one hand, three very different hilltops were examined. Roystone Rocks is made of dolomitised carboniferous limestone and resembles a lunar landscape. Here we also identified an enclosure which we believed might be a prehistoric rock-shelter. At Jackdaw Rocks, by contrast, the landscape is part dolomitised limestone and part carboniferous limestone, with a

42. Test-pitting on Roystone Rocks in search of prehistoric sites. Each person stands by a test pit measuring 0.5 x 1.0 m (photo: Graeme Barker).

Roman-period farm situated at the point where the two rock-types meet. The third hilltop, around the Lime Kiln barrow and on the edge of the barrow cemetery, may well have been a ritual landscape. On the other hand, the fourth area focussed upon the valley, in particular the natural routeway to the only spring at Roystone, immediately behind the medieval grange.

In retrospect our awareness of hilltop scatters like those at Aleck Low and Kenslow persuaded us to concentrate too much on the hilltops to the detriment of the valley. Some compensation for this bias, however, can be found in the excavations of the Romano-British dwellings in the village beyond the present Roystone Grange Farm as well as the grange excavations. In these trenches significant numbers of prehistoric lithics were found, making it possible for us to compare the patterns obtained from the valley and hilltops.

The test-pitting proceeded over several seasons, and during this time two prehistoric 'sites' were discovered. The first of these is the enclosure on Roystone Rocks. The foundations of a wall of a type otherwise unknown at Roystone (see p. 33) enclose a platform overlooking the valley that leads from Parwich to Pikehall. The back of the platform is formed by a craggy outcrop of dolomitic limestone. This area intrigued us. A test trench in the centre of the platform brought to light a distinctive Later Mesolithic microlith – a thin, elegantly worked rod made of white flint from the Lincolnshire Wolds, intended to be a barb in an arrow. Sherds of later Neolithic pottery as well as chippings from working flint and chert implements were also found. As a result we undertook more excavations. An area against the 'back wall' of the platform produced virtually the same range of objects, including an exceedingly small 'thumbnail' scraper of Later Neolithic date. Two more trenches were cut through the enclosure wall, one of which revealed sherds of a decorated Neolithic pot of so-called Grimston Ware type.

As in the case of the barrows, it appears that the history of this enclosure encompasses many millennia. Our trial excavations, like those in the Lime Kiln barrow, confirm that so much more might be clearer if the enclosure were to be totally excavated in the manner of Wigber Low. Nevertheless, this unprepossessing site may be of major importance. The Later Mesolithic flints suggest that at some time between *c.* 6000 and 3500 BC it might have been a hunting stand – a place from which game passing down the valley was observed and eventually stalked. Jeffrey Radley excavated a similar site near Sheldon, which today commands a panoramic sweep of the White Peak plateau. Like the Sheldon rock shelter, it seems that the area found a new use as the economy of the region altered. In the age of Stonehenge, *c.* 2000-1500 BC, the platform was made into an enclosure of some kind. Another enclosure of about the same date was discovered by Jeffrey

Radley on the edge of Beeley Moor, and again it was associated with monuments of great antiquity. At Roystone, the selection of long orthostats as foundation stones for the (type 5) enclosure wall indicates that this was not envisaged as some makeshift temporary use of the spot. The body of the wall may have consisted of bundles of thorns or even a drystone wall. The archaeological remains show that people occasionally broke pots and worked their tools here. The tiny scraper and the many small chippings suggest that this was a 'task site' where tools were used and repaired on the spot. One possibility is that it was a stock enclosure where from time to time skins were prepared.

The enclosure did not exist in isolation. Other small spreads of Later Neolithic pottery and lithic debris were found in test-pitting on the hill close by. In addition, with the eye of faith, it is possible to pick out several cleared patches on the west-facing hillslope beneath the enclosure. These are hardly fields in the normal sense of the word, but they could be plots that were gardened when the enclosure was in use.

The second site to be found lay close to Jackdaw Rocks where the solitary Romano-British farm called Roystone Grange 2 is situated. In 1983 the farm seemed in danger of being destroyed when Ballidon Quarry was granted permission to take away part of the hill. We therefore carried out an excavation of the Roman-period dwelling (see p. 78). Beneath the Romano-British levels some 70 flints were found, while concentrated in one corner of the trench over an area of levelled bedrock were some 80 sherds of hand-made pottery. Clearly there had been some prehistoric occupation on this spot several thousand years before the farm was built.

The flint tools belong to the Later Neolithic, and the majority were made from pebbles found in the East Midlands boulder clays. Most of the diagnostic tools are characteristic Later Neolithic scrapers (*c.* 2500-1800 BC) including short-end scrapers, long-end scrapers and a side scraper. A blade, a knife, a half-made leaf-shaped arrowhead and a completed example were also present in the assemblage. This dense concentration of implements indicates that animals were skinned and hunting tools were made here. The absence of Neolithic pottery is slightly baffling, however, and argues against any permanent settlement. In fact the pottery concentrated around the levelled bedrock belongs to a later date – the elusive Later Bronze Age (*c.* 1000-600 BC). These coarsely-made and poorly-fired jars were fabricated from clays found in the valley. Perhaps they were made only when they were needed for a purpose which remains unknown. We need to expose much more of this site if we are ever to understand it. Even so, it is worth noting that in medieval times there was a sheep-pen close to this spot (see Chapter 5), possibly where the ewes were milked, and in Victorian times a field barn was built here. In conclusion, we believe that this presently exposed hilltop has been the

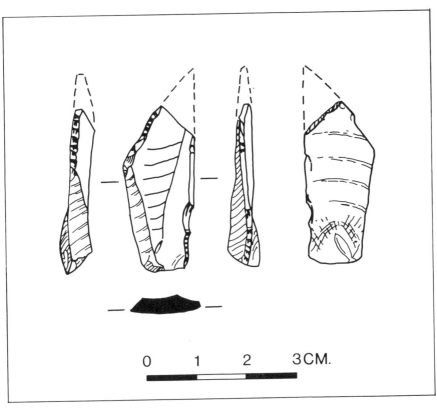

43. Creswellian point from Roystone Grange (after Terry Manby).

scene of some kind of site off and on for the past four thousand years.

The test-pitting helps us to fit these sites, all the odd scattered finds and the barrows into a picture of four thousand years of prehistoric farmers at Roystone. The prehistoric picture can be summarised as follows:

Upper Palaeolithic

Some years ago a so-called Creswellian point – a type of arrowhead made between approximately 12,000 and 10,000 BC – was found on the slope below Minninglow. This solitary discovery, together with Upper Palaeolithic flints from several caves in the Dove and Manifold valleys, attests the presence of hunters on the Derbyshire Dome long before the North Sea and English Channel existed. The pastures on the Pennines at the western end of the North European plain may have attracted herds of animals as well as hunters. Whether there was any semi-permanent occupation hereabouts at this time, such as has been discovered at Creswell in north-east Derbyshire, is a matter for speculation.

59

Later Mesolithic

Possibly as early as 6000 BC and certainly before 3500 BC small hunting groups were visiting Roystone, if not residing there. Traces of them were found not only in the enclosure on Roystone Rocks, but also in the pits dotted across the meadow beside the Parwich track. Very little remains from this period, but evidently from time to time groups occupied a sheltered niche near the spring and, from the hilltop, monitored game passing down the Parwich-Pikehall valley. Their tool kits, judging by what they lost, contained intricately chipped rods and blades known as scalene triangles. Some tools were made from white flint obtained in the Lincolnshire Wolds, though the majority were of a local chert, showing that these hunters soon appreciated how local materials could be turned to good use.

Neolithic

This is the period when Minninglow, the grandest megalithic chambered tomb known on the Peak, was built. Most of the evidence points to activities in the later Neolithic, roughly 2500-1800 BC. Concentrations of Neolithic tools and debris were found in the enclosure on Roystone Rocks, on the Roman-period farms in the valley, at Roystone Grange 2, and on the site of the medieval grange. Odd tools and discarded chippings also occurred on Roystone Rocks, but not in any significant numbers in the other three areas. Decorated Later Neolithic pottery of the so-called Beaker types was also found in the enclosure and in several of the pits on Roystone Rocks. The tools themselves are interesting. Most are made of fine transparent flint brought from the Trent Valley or the Lincolnshire Wolds. Pristine implements occur on the Roman-period sites in the valley, but most of the tools found in the enclosure had been trimmed repeatedly, leaving barely any visible trace of the cortex of the flint. These differences probably reflect different activities. The enclosure, as we have seen, may have been a task site, perhaps where stock was kept and animals were skinned. If there were dwellings it seems likely that they were in the sheltered valley where the later farms were located.

Early to Middle Bronze Age

Between *c.* 1800 and 1000 BC the barrow cemetery was created. The Collared Urns in Roystone Grange barrow 1 and the Lime Kiln barrow suggest that these mounds were built around 1800 BC. The test-pits on the hilltop around the Lime Kiln barrow, however, produced few discarded tools or chippings in contrast to the other areas where there was an uniform scatter. We can surmise from this that the landscape

44. Neolithic flint implements from Roystone (photo: Trevor Corns).

was divided into sectors, with the hill on which the barrow cemetery sits being designated by the community for its rituals, while the habitations, which have yet to be located, as well as any associated gardens and fields were distributed in the valley and western sides of the present farm. By this time local chert had replaced flint as the predominant material used by these people. Slight though the evidence is, it hints at the inception of a rather localised community with its own lithic resources and its own graveyard.

Late Bronze Age to Early Iron Age

Between *c.* 1000 and 600 BC the inhabitants of the White Peak stopped using flint and as a result become much more difficult to detect. Sherds of the crude pottery made in this period have been found in the hill-forts dotted about the region, but before the investigations at Roystone none were known from undefended homesteads. Concentrations of this type of pottery were found beneath the Romano-British site at Roystone Grange 2 and towards the southern side of the meadow beside the Parwich track. Odd sherds also turned up unexpectedly on Roystone Rocks, possibly reflecting a tradition of land use well over a millennium old.

Later Iron Age

The period between *c.* 600 BC and the arrival of the Romans in the first century AD remains an enigma. Towards the end of this period the White Peak lay in the zone between the Coritani, a tribe controlling the East Midlands, and the warlike Brigantes, who dominated much of

45. Excavation of the Neolithic buildings at Lismore Fields, Buxton (courtesy of the Trent & Peak Archaeological Trust).

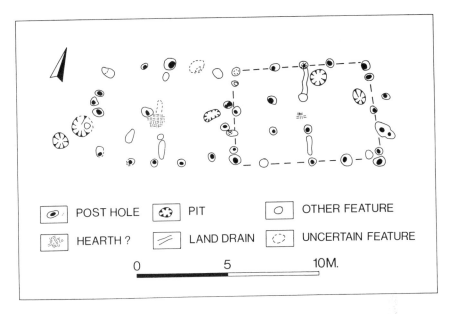

| POST HOLE | PIT | OTHER FEATURE |
| HEARTH ? | LAND DRAIN | UNCERTAIN FEATURE |

0   5   10M.

46. Plan of the Neolithic buildings found at Lismore Fields, Buxton (after Daryll Garton).

north-eastern England. The diagnostic pottery of these peoples has not been found in the White Peak, though occasional sporadic finds from hill-forts and caves demonstrate conclusively that the region was not entirely abandoned. Absolutely nothing was found in the test-pitting to shed light on this enigma. Perhaps the crude Later Bronze Age jars continued to be used in this out-of-the-way place, though the discovery of a solitary typical Late Iron Age rimsherd in a cutting through a field bank (see p. 80) suggests that this is unlikely.

This archaeological sequence begs many questions. In particular, we are unable confidently to reconstruct the long transition from the Mesolithic to the Iron Age with any reference to the environmental history. Tell-tale environmental data simply do not survive at Roystone. There are no buried soils that might help us to reconstruct the quality of the prehistoric soils; similarly mollusca, which might help us to form a picture of the White Peak habitat, are also absent; and there is no opportunity to obtain cores containing pollen samples that might reveal the vegetational history of the area. Finally, animal bones and carbonised botanical remains such as cereals or weeds have long since perished in the acidic limestone soils. We therefore need to fit the information provided by the Roystone investigations into the picture for the Peak District as a whole. This picture, though made up of many disparate pieces, nevertheless has a compelling cohesion. It brings us to the unlikely conclusion that for at least one millennium of our history this region was one of the most pre-eminent in Britain.

3. Four Thousand Years of Prehistoric Farming
A prehistoric farmhouse at Roystone?

No traces of a prehistoric house were discovered at Roystone. If one existed, it probably lay near the spring where the Cistercian grange was later built, or on the hillside by the present farmhouse. Fortunately we do have some idea of what such a building might have looked like at the time when the barrow cemetery was in use. Excavations between 1984 and 1986 at Lismore Fields, a meadow on the outskirts of Buxton, unexpectedly revealed a number of buildings close to a spring. Only the holes for the posts supporting the building were found, but these are sufficient for us to form an impression of a prehistoric Peakland farmhouse. As at Roystone, traces of Later Mesolithic occupation were found at Lismore Fields. A radiocarbon date pinpointed this phase to 5220 ± 80 bc. The principal building, however, belongs to the Later Neolithic age. It was a small rectangular structure measuring 5 × 4 metres. The rectangle was divided into two compartments with a hearth set between them. Associated with this building are the remains of other rectangular buildings and of a circular structure just over 4 metres in diameter. As at Roystone, hundreds of flint chippings, flint implements and potsherds were associated with the settlement.

A building of this kind would take some finding at Roystone, but this chance discovery at Lismore Fields gives us an idea of the sort of farmhouses associated with barrow-building and pastoralism in the Peak during the age of Stonehenge. Such a building, it is worth noting, had barely half the floor-area of the Romano-British dwellings found at Roystone and other Peakland sites, and was also only about half the size of a medieval peasant's cottage. Of course, this rare discovery may not be typical of Neolithic dwellings. Indeed, despite the presence of a hearth, it may not have been a permanent dwelling at all. But for the moment it is all we have to go on, and it obviously poses as many intriguing questions as it answers.

Roystone in regional perspective

The Romans arrived in Britain less than two thousand years ago. About four thousand years before that there were hunters camping near the spring at Roystone. This time-span in some ways defies our imagination, but it is critical if we are to understand the prehistory of the Peak.

By about 10,000 BC hunters were present on this high ground. They occasionally lost their arrowheads, such as the elegantly-fashioned Creswellian point found near Minninglow. Perhaps they were seasonal visitors, tracking herds that migrated to the high ground out of the thickly forested North Sea plain. This is unlikely to have been an isolated episode, and hunters probably continued to visit the Derbyshire Dome long after the North Sea had taken shape. By the Later Mesolithic hunters were regular visitors and had possibly even settled in many parts of the Peak. They were no longer just using the caves as their forebears had done, but clearly making hunting stands from which to monitor game. The hunting stand at Roystone, in common with a number known from other parts of the Peak, reflects the gradual intensification of human activity in the region. This is also illustrated by the tools they used after *c.* 6000 BC, when local cherts were employed to make fine burins, scrapers and points – tools that had hitherto been fashioned from white flint brought from the Lincolnshire or Yorkshire Wolds. This indicates that these people were becoming less mobile. They may even have cultivated small plots of ground, raising herds and establishing, it might be argued, the first farming presence at Roystone.

The real character of the Later Mesolithic activity at Roystone remains an intriguing enigma. It is unlikely, though, that these hunters were colonists in the accepted sense of the term. They represent instead the last of a long tradition of mobile peoples and perhaps the first to take advantage of the pastoral qualities of the landscape.

How we interpret these first farmers largely depends upon what the landscape itself looked like. Were there open pastures as they are today, or was it more wooded? The open hills of Roystone make it difficult to imagine it could ever have looked different, but the wooded valleys leading down to Cromford a few miles to the east remind us that this need not necessarily have been open country. The only environmental evidence comes from the unique discovery of buried soils beneath a Bronze Age site at Parwich. Professor G.W. Dimbleby analysed these soils and found that they contained sufficient pollen grains to allow him to reconstruct the surrounding landscape. He proposed that the immediate vicinity was open grassland dominated by various grasses and plantain. Traces of herbs and cereals were also identified, as were hazel and alder. By the Bronze Age, Dimbleby concluded, the hilltops were open pastures where limited cereal cultivation was practised, but patches of woodland and scrub, much as today, grew nearby. Thus tracts of upland may have been exposed by the Later Mesolithic period, but the valleys were in all probability still thickly wooded.

We must also consider the question of climate. As Britain became an island, its weather shifted from a Continental to a more Oceanic type. This led to an amelioration of the climate after *c.* 6000 BC which was most apparent in upland regions. Mean summer temperatures were almost 1°C higher in 4000 than they had been in 6000 BC, and the difference in winter was nearly 2°C. This minor climatic optimum

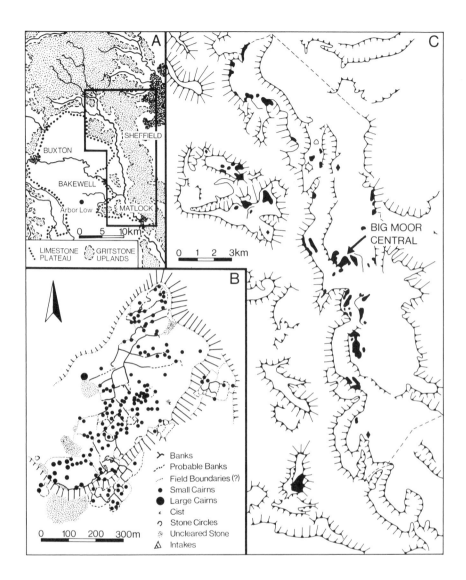

47. Remains of Bronze Age field systems on the East Moors. Each of the black areas shown on map C relates to preserved field systems. Map B illustrates the example of Big Moor Central (after John Barnatt).

came to an end around 3000 BC, but by this time some settlers may have established themselves in valleys like Roystone, as we have seen, and in summer the pastures may have attracted shepherds from the valleys to the south and east. Between 3500 and 2000 BC, after this optimum, Peakland farmers were probably few in number, but they almost certainly established an imprint upon the landscape that was

66

48. Remains of Bronze Age dwellings on Big Moor (photo: Ray Manley).

to endure for many millennia. In this period, for example, the first ritual monument was constructed at Gib Hill alongside the henge at Arbor Low. Here was perhaps the first cathedral of these people. It was to evolve, much as our cathedrals have done, over as many as fifteen centuries, serving as the hub of a network of ritual monuments dotted about the high points of the Peak. Quite possibly some simple earthen prototype may have been constructed before the megalithic chambered cairn at Minninglow, marking this part of the plateau as the property of a certain tribe.

The soils from the Bronze Age barrow at Parwich analysed by Professor Dimbleby show that by the second millennium BC the climate had again warmed appreciably. Some climatologists estimate that in the age of Stonehenge the summer temperatures were 2-3°C warmer, much as in the eleventh and twelfth centuries AD. All over Britain there was an explosion of activity, leading to a tremendous growth in the population. Nowhere is this clearer than in the Peak District. Arbor Low and the Bull Ring seem to have become the focal points for two tribes between 2000 and 1500 BC, and large numbers of new settlements augmented by summer pastoralists are attested by the evidence. Roystone fits comfortably into this picture. On the one hand there were perhaps farmers residing in the valley who built the barrows. On the other, the veneer of lithic debris across the landscape almost certainly betrays the passage of the mobile shepherds. The cereal pollen from the Parwich soil samples supports the view that hardy crops were being cultivated, possibly in small plots sufficient to support households. Meanwhile the pastures were used by large herds of animals which, to judge from later Celtic sources, became the real currency of this increasingly complex economy. With time, as one might expect, the many influences from other regions were supplanted by those developed locally. Hence local cherts were preferred to imported flints and local ornamentation began to feature on the funerary pots in which cremated remains were placed.

It is easy to underestimate the scale of this expansion. It took place four thousand years ago and, apart from Arbor Low, the archaeology is highly ephemeral. However, as with the Roman period in the Peak, we should take note of circumstances at their most marginal. Not only do Later Neolithic/Early Bronze Age objects occur commonly in the test-pits at Roystone, but more significantly large numbers of fields from this date have been discovered on the moorlands on the eastern side of the Peak. In an important study of these fields and farms, John Barnatt has shown convincingly that they represent the final climax of demographic expansion in the region at about 1500 BC, when marginal land was brought into horticultural use and herders began to take advantage of these areas. Barnatt's painstaking surveys of the remnant farms lead him tentatively to estimate that as many as 7,000 people may have inhabited the East Moors in the Bronze Age. This zone, which is barely inhabited today, makes up less than a sixth of the total area of the Peak. The dangers of using rough approximations are obvious, but taking Barnatt's estimate as a rough guide we might guess that six times this number occupied the Peak District as a whole – in short, a population approximating to the 38,000 who live there today!

Later in the second millennium the climate began to deteriorate. This must have caused considerable hardship for the most marginally-placed inhabitants of the region. At the same time these thin upland soils could not have sustained many centuries of use. From what we know about conditions there in post-medieval times, it was very easy to over-graze the pastures. The surveyor William Farey points out that plenty of lime fertiliser was needed. Indeed, with the agricultural revolution many White Peak pastures were reseeded. In these circumstances no stretch of the imagination is needed to appreciate how a region that had been a core area of Britain could be reduced to a backwater. By the end of the millennium very different

49. Reconstruction of a prehistoric encampment on Roystone Rocks (drawing: Simon Manby).

kinds of settlements had been established. Hillforts such as Ball's Cross at Bakewell, Fin Cop above Monsal Dale and Mam Tor overlooking the Hope Valley indicate the inception of large communities conscious of defence. Evidently the whole pattern of life was altering. Competition for local lead needed for making bronze implements may have brought greater strife to the area and led to the construction of communal fortifications. There was certainly a staggering depopulation of the region, convincingly attested by the desertion of the East Moors. But not everyone disappeared. The later Bronze Age concentrations of potsherds found at Roystone demonstrate emphatically for the first time that some small-scale habitations persisted on the White Peak.

The demographic downswing did not end there. The virtual absence of Iron Age archaeology from the Peak District is in complete contrast to the density of second-millennium activity. Over the course of several centuries the personality of the region had irrevocably altered. In these circumstances we cannot doubt that the woodland and scrub expanded to recolonise some of the pastures, leaving only the hilltops exposed. Collections of Iron Age objects from caves at Harborough Rocks and in Dimmin's Dale indicate the continued presence of shepherds in the summer, following a tradition several millennia old. But in contrast to the formation of densely populated, complex kingdoms in the lowlands of late prehistoric Britain, the Peak seems to have been virtually unoccupied. This helps to explain what happened when the Romans arrived in the region.

4

Pioneers of the Roman Age

> On any Roman Britain site the impression that constantly haunts the archaeologist, like a bad smell or a stickiness on the fingers, is that of an ugliness which pervades the place like a London fog: not merely the common vulgar ugliness of the Roman Empire, but a blundering stupid ugliness that cannot even rise to the level of that vulgarity.
>
> R.G. Collingwood & J.N.L. Myers, *Roman Britain and the English Settlements* (1936)

Collingwood's disparaging view of the provincialism of Roman Britain continues to have a wide currency. Great architecture and art are undeniably missing from Roman Britain, but its material remains are far from negligible. Such attitudes, however, have not been restricted to scholars. In the 1850s Bateman's long-time associate, Samuel Carrington, uncharacteristically devoted many days to an excavation of a Romano-British village at Wetton above the Manifold Valley. At one point in his unusually long report on this dig, Carrington describes it as the 'very Pompeii of North Staffordshire'. Then, commenting upon the 'vacant aboriginal mind' that etched a primitive gaming board on a limestone slab, he asks: 'How could these people exist without their stimulating Sunday paper?' To be fair, Carrington's ten-page excavation report, published in 1861, illustrates the seriousness with which he had undertaken this dig. He was evidently surprised by the size of the Roman-period settlement and its material wealth.

Archaeologists all over England, indeed all over the Empire, have now come to terms with such discoveries. The forum at Rome may be magnificent, but the real testimony to Rome's grandeur lies in the immense intensification of farming across its provinces, and the meshing together of these hitherto disparate regions into a coherent economic community. The scale and extent of Roman influence in the Peak District should therefore come as no surprise.

Roman legions reached the Peak District in the mid-50s AD, when Nero was Emperor and Didius Gallus was governor of Britain. Historians believe that the Peak lay between the territory of the Coritani in the East Midlands, who were favourably disposed to the

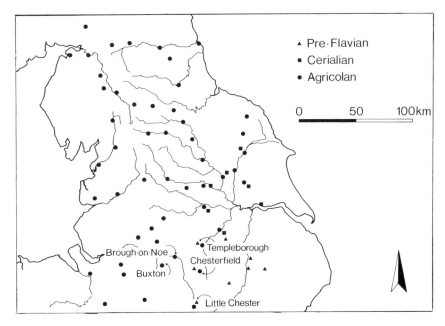

50. Early Roman forts in the north Midlands and northern England.

Romans, and the warlike Brigantes to the North. Its sparse population may have been only loosely affiliated to either of these tribes, making it easy prey for the Romans. The Roman advance had been prompted by the threat posed to the province by the Brigantian King Venutius and his Queen Cartimandua. Tacitus records that Gallus sent auxiliaries north to counter the Brigantian threat. When matters did not improve, he sent the ninth legion north under the command of Caesius Nasica. Forts were constructed at Chesterfield and Templeborough (now a northern suburb of Sheffield). In the short term, Gallus' policy worked. The Brigantes remained inactive while Boudicca raised her infamous revolt in the south. They were eventually overpowered by Petillius Cerialis in AD 71-4, leaving northern Britain as far as the Tyne-Solway line in Roman hands.

The prime concern of the Roman conquest was to obtain resources, primarily minerals. In the first decade after the invasion the military were prospecting for lead in the Mendips and for tin in Cornwall. The advance as far north as the river Don in the mid-50s secured the Peak from Brigantian depredations, and before the end of the century lead extraction was being carried out in the fort at Brough-on-Noe in the Hope Valley. Lead pigs associated with the region, stamped with the letters LVT or LVTVD, or in one case LVTVDARES, are associated with a lost place called Lutudarum. Some pigs are also stamped with the letters EX ARG, suggesting that silver had been removed from the ore. This has intrigued students of Peakland lead mining as the local

51. Gritstone altar found in the grounds of Haddon Hall. The inscription reads: *Deo Marti Braciacae Quintus Sittius Caecilianus praefectus cohortis I Aquitanorum votum solvit* (To the god Mars Braciaca, Quintus Sittius Caecilianus, prefect of the First Cohort of Aquitanians, fulfilled his vow).

52. Lead pig from Tansley Moor, found in 1894. The ingot is inscribed as the property of Publius Rubrius Abascantus, a mining concessionaire of Lutudarum (courtesy of the British Museum).

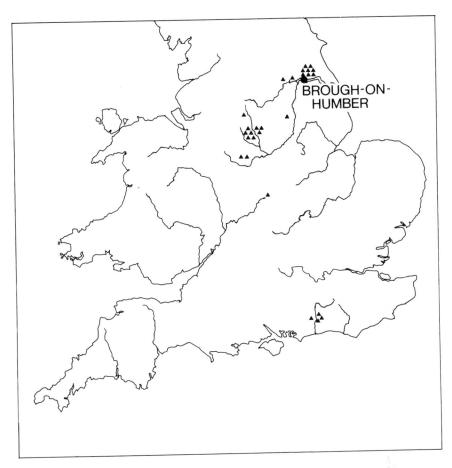

53. Finds of Derbyshire lead pigs in Britain. The number of discoveries from Brough-on-Humber suggests that the lead was exported to the Continent from this port.

ore appears to be low in silver, though in the eighteenth century there were silver mines at Ball Eye near Bonsall and Masson Hill near Matlock. A few pigs were not stamped at all. The pigs weigh up to 170 lbs (77 kg), though smaller examples have been found. Lutudarum itself has long intrigued historians, though its location has now been pin-pointed with some confidence, as we shall see. As long as monumental buildings needed lead for gutters, pipes and roofing, and as more and more private bath-houses were constructed in villas, the Peakland lead industry, like its counterparts in Flintshire and the Mendips, was bound to flourish.

The Romans were concerned with other resources too. Surveys made by archaeologists in East Anglia, Wessex and the Midlands show that the later Iron Age economy of Britain was expanding rapidly on the eve of the Roman invasion. Based upon the fields laid out in the Early

54. The phase 1 aisled farm (house 1) at Roystone Grange, showing the post-holes and post-pits (photo: Richard Hodges).

Bronze Age, it seems that large tracts of the British landscape were intensively farmed. The Roman agronomists clearly appreciated the productive merits of the island, and with considerable vision extended the limits of cultivation and farming to embrace almost all parts of the province. Cash-cropping, much as the EEC has fostered in recent times, suited the needs of the Empire, and for a short time at least was favoured by its treasury. This was the context in which the Romano-British village at Roystone grew up.

The Romano-British village

The platform we discovered on our first visit to Roystone on that wild March day in 1978 (see p. 3) is the largest of a cluster of four or five dwellings on the east-facing slope, a little to the north of the present Roystone Grange Farm. In addition, a second Romano-British settlement (known as Roystone Grange 2) occupies the hill beside Jackdaw Rocks, a kilometre to the south of the village. We have excavated the large platform (house 1) and put a trench through its associated yard, as well as trenching two other dwellings in the village. At Roystone Grange 2, as mentioned in Chapter 3, we have excavated

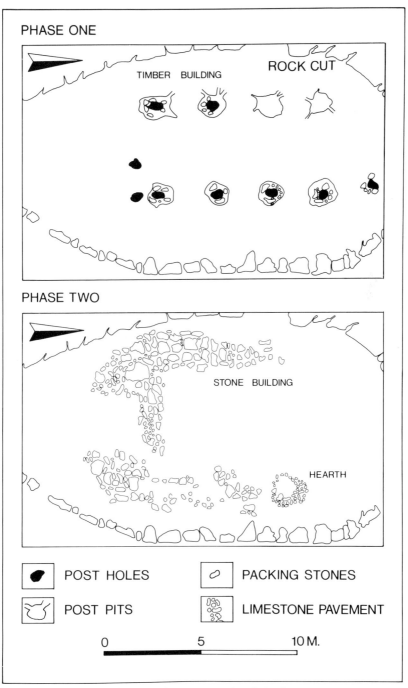

PHASE ONE

TIMBER BUILDING

ROCK CUT

PHASE TWO

STONE BUILDING

HEARTH

⬤ POST HOLES   ⬠ PACKING STONES

🜄 POST PITS   ▦ LIMESTONE PAVEMENT

0   5   10 M.

55. House 1 at Roystone Grange: phase 1, second and third centuries; phase 2, fourth century.

half the house platform and trenched the associated yard. As a result of these excavations we can begin to form an impression of the history of these farm-buildings.

House 1 has a long history and may have been the equivalent of the manor in the village. It was constructed on a platform about 20 metres long and 12 metres broad, revetted by large dolomitic boulders. It lies within a enclosure, part of which is a double-orthostat (type 4) wall. In the north-east corner of the enclosure lay a dew-pond and possibly a spring. A young woman had been inhumed in the soft white sands of the pond, and a second body was discovered close by in 1947 when the milking parlour was put up here. The excavations of the house showed that it was a two-period building. The earliest building was a large, sub-rectangular, aisled farmhouse of a kind that is better known from the Midlands and is often regarded as the prototype for a villa. (Later still, an aisled building of precisely this size served as the principal hall inside South Cadbury Camp (Somerset) during the fifth century AD; it has been associated with the mythical King Arthur.) The building had at least three bays supported by substantial posts which would have taken the main weight of the roof. Fragmentary traces of drystone walls were found on the east side, but the shape of the dwelling could be inferred from the deliberate shaving of natural limestone to fit the building on its north-west corner. Very little material remained inside the building to help us interpret its lay-out, but a bronze *as* of the second consulship of Domitian dating to AD 77 was found in a thin layer of undisturbed stratigraphy. From the layer sealing the building we discovered a number of sherds of fine Samian Ware bowls (made in central France), but the majority of the discarded pottery is a coarse local type known as Derbyshire Ware. Fragments of tablewares coated in coloured slips made in the Trent and Nene valleys make up the remainder of the ceramics found in the excavations.

It seems that the aisled hall was demolished about AD 250-300. The post-pits and post-holes in which the aisle-posts had stood were back-filled, and a layer of earth and refuse was spread over the site. On top of this a curious structure made of selected limestone slabs was built. The slabs formed a H-shape, and one arm terminated in a hearth in which lead debris was discovered. Whether the slabs indicate the footings of a turf or low drystone wall, or whether they are all that remain of a floor surface is a question that continues to intrigue us. Samuel Carrington first discovered slab surfaces like this one in his excavations at Borough Fields, Wetton, and others have been identified in small-scale excavations of Romano-British house-sites elsewhere in the Peak. In fact, slab surfaces occur on all the other Romano-British sites at Roystone. Furthermore, the bay containing the byre in the twelfth/thirteenth-century grange also had a slab floor, and large sections of the drystone wall were built on top of slabs! The

56. The phase 2 house is indicated by the limestone paving-slabs (the scales are 2 m long) (photo: Richard Hodges).

hearth beyond the eastern wall at house 1, though, poses a further problem. Is it of later date? Was it for lead-smelting? Sadly, it was directly below the turf and it proved impossible to determine its stratigraphic relationship to the adjacent slab wall. One point is clear, however: the slab-based building was smaller than the earlier one and represents a major change in the vernacular architecture at Roystone.

About 50 metres to the south, along the hillside, a second, smaller dwelling (house 2) was trenched. This building was probably about 15 metres long and 6 metres wide, with a yard in front, and traces of an enclosure wall, as though it was a clearly defined unit like house 1. The sequence appears to be the same as that found in house 1. The earliest building was raised on a platform cut into the hillside, and after some centuries demolished and replaced by a building in which limestone slabs were used. A third-century bronze *as* shows that the demolition of the first building belongs to the period after *c*. AD 250. A fine bronze pin, a jet ring and a dolphin brooch dated to the early second century AD were found in the demolition level separating the two phases of occupation. A third dwelling can be plainly seen some 40 metres to the south, and a fourth with a small walled farmyard was examined a little higher up the slope.

Unlike many Romano-British peasant dwellings known from the Midlands, there was no trace of a preceding Iron Age house on the site of any of these buildings. Moreover each dwelling, as far as we can tell,

57. Second-century dolphin brooch found in the excavations of house 2 in the village at Roystone (photo: Trevor Corns).

was rebuilt in the third century in an entirely different form and then remained unaltered until it was abandoned.

The exception to this rule proved to be the solitary farm known as Roystone Grange 2 on Jackdaw Rocks. The platform on which the house once stood is now home to many rabbits. An excavation of half of it showed that in many ways it was identical to the smaller dwellings (2, 3 & 4) in the village nearby. Like them, it was set in an enclosure, in this case made of a particularly well-preserved stretch of double-orthostat walling. Traces of an outhouse or ancillary building can be seen tucked up against the enclosure wall. Roystone Grange 2 was not a new site, however. Neolithic flints and a concentration of Late Bronze Age potsherds showed that it had been a settlement site on and off for two thousand years (see p. 58) before Roman-period settlers constructed a substantial dwelling here.

Roman-period Roystone probably comprised more than five farms. It is likely that the present farmhouse sits on top of at least one, and yet others may await discovery. At the moment we have little understanding of the internal arrangements of these houses, but we must assume that no more than half – and quite possibly less – was used to house livestock. Even so, some rough estimates of the population of Roystone can be calculated using the farms as a rough guide. The most commonly used calculation is that of the anthropologist R. Naroll, who considers that in peasant societies each person requires 0.10 m^2 of floor space. At Roystone this would mean about 12 people occupying half the aisled building (house 1), and at least 4-5 people in each of the other farms. This would mean that from the second century Roystone supported over 30 people in the village and a further 5 or more in the outlying farm. This estimate is likely to be on the low side, and a figure as high as 50 is not unlikely. Quite clearly, a population of 30-50 is well above the level that could be safely supported by the land.

The farms themselves, of course, tell only part of the story. The way in which Roystone was farmed should reveal how it could support a permanent population of this size. The discovery of type 4 double-orthostat field walls as well as field banks associated with the village enables us to reconstruct the economy of the community. As we saw in Chapter 2, sufficient traces of the foundations of these walls survive to show that two large blocks of land were enclosed when the villagers arrived. The two blocks lie either side of the valley, through which ran a Roman-period track (preserved as a holloway in the field south of the grange). The track resembles the pencil-thin body of a butterfly, the enclosed areas being its wings. The northern wing covers about 30 hectares and contains the cluster of dwellings, each possibly set in its own enclosure. This area generally encompasses rocky dolomitised limestone, but on the east-facing slope above the farms there are several cleared patches covering about 1,500 square metres. By contrast, the eastern wing covers a section of the carboniferous limestone within which there is an outcrop of dolomitic limestone. This enclosure too is about 30 hectares in area. At its highest point lies the Lime Kiln barrow excavated by Barry Marsden, where an inhumation with an associated pin and dolphin brooch (like that from house 2) was discovered. This wing also contains three discrete remains of field banks dating from this period. The best-preserved lie on a steep west-facing slope known as the Walk where the banks parcel up natural terracing into small plots (see p. 34). The unmistakable undulations of lazy-beds, the result of spade cultivation, were observed within this field system on one occasion when the sun was low in the sky. The steepness of the slope and the thin soils make it likely that the plots were a short-term measure, perhaps made just after the area had been cleared of vegetation. The edge bank of a second set of fields runs along the top of the scarp overlooking the present farm, and then turns as though heading towards the Lime Kiln barrow. This bank has been preserved because later farmers in subsequent times have never ploughed so close to this steep edge. In one of the three cuttings through this bank three tiny abraded sherds of mid-second-century Samian Ware were found. The third set of fields lies on the valley side. An excavation showed that the highly accentuated banks that we see today were divisions between linear plots about 40 metres wide.

Romano-British field systems cover lowland Britain like a great net. Miles of fields arranged like bricks in a wall, for instance, have been plotted by aerial photography in Nottinghamshire. At Roystone, however, it is the investment in walling that catches the imagination. The double-orthostat walls wriggle around numerous obstacles that have long since disappeared. Yet wherever we have put cuttings through these walls there have been good footings. The villagers evidently ensured that these were solid, and wall-builders ever since have saluted their achievement by re-using them. This makes their wriggling alignment all the more curious. One explanation may be that the walls were erected through scrubland and even recently cleared woods.

Three other features help us to interpret the landscape at this time. The first is a paddock made of double-orthostat walling which is comparatively well preserved. It measures 20 × 7 metres and lies in the bottom of the valley, 30 metres or so south of the modern sheep-pens. It could have held up to fifty sheep, or rather fewer cattle. It lies at the narrowest point in the valley, into which the animals might be driven. Around it, a few metres to the east, swerves a deeply-cut track – a holloway which probably belongs to this period. The holloway would have linked Roystone to Ballidon and other points south.

The second feature is a holloway of prehistoric or Roman date half-way up the south-facing slope of Roystone Rocks. A bank defines the south side of the holloway, and on top of this runs a stretch of double-orthostat (type 4) walling (Fig. 32). The bank itself has been clearly accentuated by the holloway and is earlier in date than the wall. Air photographs show the faintest trace of the track as it descends the slope and heads in the direction of the present track (and footpath) on the far side of the valley that leads to Minninglow. These photographs also show that the orthostat wall runs along the bank, and then turns southwards down the slope from the point where the bank terminates. Once it leaves the bank, the wall wriggles as though passing through open woodland. Did the bank mark the upslope edge of the woodland, alongside which ran an ancient track that also proved useful in Roman times? Might it have been a way across the southern fringes of the White Peak, much as Gallowlow Lane was to be in medieval times?

The third feature was found in the angle formed by the bank and orthostat wall. Here a trench was excavated across the seemingly levelled ground. This showed that a lead rake – a small shaft about 1.5 metres deep and about 1 metre across – had been cut through a lead vein. The lead and fluorspar in which it was embedded had been methodically crushed on the site and the spoil tossed either side of the hole. When the vein was emptied the rake was filled in and stones firmly embedded in its upper level to prevent it subsiding. The soil thrown out to the north pre-dates the bank beside the holloway, over which the orthostat wall runs. This shows that the rake probably pre-dates the construction of the walled enclosures in the second century. To make matters more intriguing, when a small cutting was made through the wall where it rises over the bank a solitary sherd of

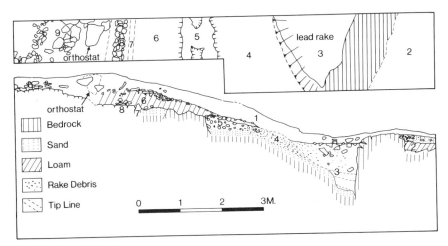

58. Plan and section through the lead quarry pit (rake) found in Trench VIIc.

poorly-made Later Iron Age pottery was found buried below the orthostat foundations. Pottery of this kind is scarce in the Peak District, but was probably in circulation up to the second century when the production of mass-produced Derbyshire Ware began. It is tempting, therefore, to interpret the bank as a boundary beside a late prehistoric or early Roman lead-prospecting area. There are no other signs of lead rakes on this sector of the slope, though about 40 metres westwards along the holloway there are several deep shafts that appear to be of a post-medieval type.

Did the early Roman mineral prospectors cover up their activities? A geophysical survey made with a proton magnetometer of the fields around the Lime Kiln barrow on the opposite hill strongly suggests that lead rakes have also been filled in there. As these fields were used in Romano-British and medieval times, it is tempting to ascribe these geophysical results to prehistoric or early Roman lead exploration. Still more shafts may have existed in the area of the village. Aerial photographs show a strange anomaly, rather like an irregular scar, crossing the slope where farms 3 and 4 were located.

A reconstruction of the Romano-British farm

In the light of the archaeological evidence Roystone in the Roman period can be divided into three phases:

(1) exploration before colonisation
(2) colonisation
(3) recession and desertion.

4. Pioneers of the Roman Age

Exploration before colonisation

The evidence for this phase is very slight. Only the lead rake and the holloway beside it might be attributed to this time, but it is possible that both features are in fact prehistoric. One other related aspect needs to be taken into account. The wriggling line of the double-orthostat walls is best explained as a response to the existence of trees and bushes, and suggests that the vegetation in the valley and on the hillsides at Roystone may have regenerated since Bronze Age times. Likewise the walled enclosures in the form of a butterfly spreading its wings give the impression of a farming regime imposed upon the landscape. It looks like the work of colonists rather than Iron Age farmers adapting to the new values of the Roman age. This interpretation, however, is certain to be controversial.

The colonisation of Roystone, of course, represents no more than an episode in the Roman conquest of the Peak District. The Iron Age population of this region, or rather its virtual absence, is obviously an important factor. Nevertheless, historians have tentatively attempted to explain tribal circumstances in the region when the Romans arrived. Some time ago, for instance, Sir Ian Richmond proposed that the Peak District was occupied by a tribe (a *sept*) affiliated to but perhaps not part of the Brigantes. More recently, as evidence of Neronian forts at Chesterfield and Templeborough has come to light, historians have favoured the idea that this was a buffer zone between the Brigantes to the north of the river Don, and the Coritani south and east of the limits of the White Peak. Either way, the Derbyshire Dome was a backwater that may have boasted its own upland traditions dating back to Neolithic times. Its resources cannot have gone unnoticed by the mineral surveyors who accompanied the Roman military advance.

It is likely that, in common with the Mendips, the evaluation of the mineral and agrarian potential of the area was made from the Roman military bases. Between c. AD 55 and 120, the Roman government must have been able to form a useful if restricted impression of the Peak. As the only evidence for the Later Iron Age comes from cave sites (see p. 69) almost certainly associated with shepherds, it is probable that the Romans first formed a perspective of the White Peak from those hill-tops that were still grazed. Regeneration of vegetation since Bronze Age times, especially in the valleys, would have limited the scope of the Roman land surveyors. They must therefore have been dependent upon existing trackways to assemble their information. It is not hard to imagine that their reports urged the economic sense of clearing and making use of the land.

Colonisation

Several factors may have encouraged the colonisation of the region. Any alteration in the climate, for instance, must be taken into account. The climatic deterioration of *c*. 1200-600 BC had involved both a decline in mean temperature and an increase in rainfall. Temperature then rose marginally to about 1°C above the present level from the Later Iron Age until the end of the Roman period. Rainfall probably declined from the fourth/third centuries BC until the fourth century AD. As we have seen, this may well have made a considerable difference to living conditions in the region. Barley as well as oats could be grown in these circumstances, and the longer growing season would invariably have provided a larger hay-crop to sustain livestock through the winter months.

Social factors are more difficult to calculate. Field surveys and excavations in Lincolnshire, Northamptonshire and Nottinghamshire emphatically show the phenomenal impact of the Romans upon lowland areas of Britain. New villages, great networks of field systems, and the colonisation and cultivation of areas such as the Lincolnshire Fens and the thick woodlands of Warwickshire all began to take shape in the late first century AD. Agricultural intensification created its own social momentum, necessitating more hands to work on the land. This led in turn to a rapid growth of the rural population. The strains on traditional Celtic society must have been immense as the community adapted itself on the one hand to Roman taxation, and on the other to an incipient materialism induced by new industries and highly effective marketing. The sociology of these circumstances has not been recorded, but parallels for it can be found in the Third World today as traditional societies are enveloped by a truly global economy.

But how were farmers induced to settle at Roystone and where did they come from?

Historians favour treating the Peak District as an imperial estate in the first and second centuries AD, where the mining of lead was administered by a local government official. On other estates in the Empire, the government tended to attract settlers by offering leases at low rentals. In the Peakland case, settlers were needed to colonise the ground, and to begin the process of mining and farming which with time might yield through taxation a good return to the state. The government administrator was probably based at Lutudarum, the place referred to on the lead pigs produced in the region. Until recently this centre eluded archaeologists, but in 1980 excavations in advance of making a reservoir near Carsington (about 8 kilometres south-east of Roystone) revealed traces of a large settlement, quite unlike the familiar farming communities of the Peak, with a modest villa close by. The discovery of a hoard of lead pigs at the settlement site further supports the widely-held opinion that this was the place to which all

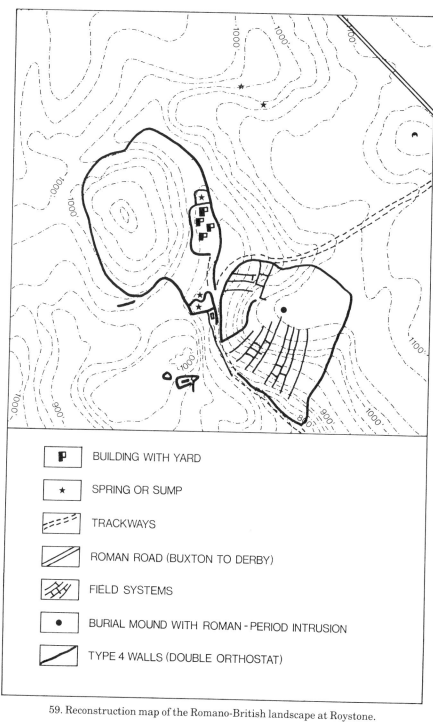

P — BUILDING WITH YARD

★ — SPRING OR SUMP

═══ — TRACKWAYS

⬛ — ROMAN ROAD (BUXTON TO DERBY)

⬛ — FIELD SYSTEMS

● — BURIAL MOUND WITH ROMAN-PERIOD INTRUSION

⬛ — TYPE 4 WALLS (DOUBLE ORTHOSTAT)

59. Reconstruction map of the Romano-British landscape at Roystone.

the local farmers brought their lead. Here it would have been weighed and purchased by the state before being stamped and despatched, sometimes to Continental destinations.

But lead was not the only resource to be exploited on the White Peak. The traditional use of this landscape for running sheep will not have gone unnoticed by the Roman government. Pennine fleeces were not of the highest quality but, as in medieval times, they were probably in demand on the Continent. The combination of two cash crops – lead and wool – certainly proved attractive to a group of settlers. The aisled farm at Roystone (house 1), resembling the dwellings of the emergent rural elite in the Midlands, lends support to the speculation that an entire community from the Trent Valley or further south may have accepted the favourable terms offered by the local procurator.

The worn fragments of Samian Ware bowls found in the excavations of the dwellings as well as in the fields indicates that the colonisation began in the early second century AD. A massive amount of labour was invested in the new venture. Smaller walls, like the remains from the Bronze Age on the East Moors (see p. 68), would have been adequate to enclose much of this land. Instead, the double-orthostat variety was used, with its foundations, its rubble core, and the apparent fashioning of the orthostats in some cases, revealing a purposeful attempt to define the bounds of the land.

The lay-out of the farm shows that the dwellings lay close together in the lee of Roystone Rocks, alongside the track through the valley. The western enclosure around Roystone Rocks may have been used as an infield in which stock were kept during the winter months, and where there were a few plots of cultivated ground. The other enclosure was largely cultivated. The 30 hectares seem to have been divided up by simple linear banks into small plots and larger fields. Beyond the enclosed areas lay open pastures – the commons – where sheep and to a lesser extent cattle might graze in the summer.

Several features of this farm merit closer scrutiny. First, the valley became the principal axis of communication between Roystone and other Romano-British communities at Pikehall and Ballidon. This axis appears to have replaced the holloway that crossed the southern fringe of the White Peak by way of Minninglow (see p. 80). Doubtless the track to Minninglow continued to be used, as it was a direct route to the metalled Roman road, known in medieval times as The Street, that ran between Buxton and Derby on the far side of the barrow. Secondly, it appears that the enclosures were designed for collective use by the community, though at some later date Roystone Grange 2 was built outside the original bounds of the colonised landscape. Thirdly, the huge effort put into making this agrarian landscape seems unnecessary unless there was some other dimension to the property that was uppermost in the minds of the colonists, but is largely hidden

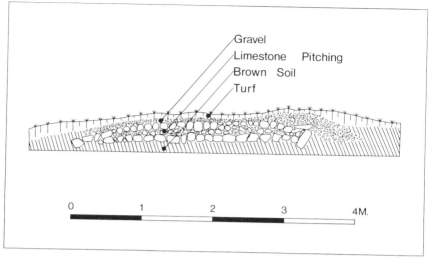

Gravel
Limestone   Pitching
Brown Soil
Turf

0   1   2   3   4M.

60. Section through the Roman road, known as 'The Street' near Minninglow (after John Lomas).

from our view. Why, for instance, did the infield need to be so securely enclosed? Wouldn't simple boulder walls have been sufficient to prevent stock from penetrating the cultivated ground in the eastern enclosure? These questions cannot be answered with any certainty. We can only propose that the settlers wished to signal to others the value they placed on their newly cleared land. It seems likely, though, that they were defining their landscape *before* they could see it as an entity. In other words, they set out the boundaries before the vegetation cover was removed. This leads us to speculate that the enclosed areas had already been identified by mineral prospectors as valuable zones. Perhaps other lead rakes criss-cross the area, invisible to our eyes – in contrast to the scars left after post-medieval mining – because in Roman times, for reasons that are not at all clear, it was deemed necessary to fill them in.

The pattern of walled enclosures found at Roystone is not common in the White Peak, but this may be simply because no one has looked for them. Most of the Romano-British farming communities in the region are typically associated with enclosures for penning flocks of sheep. Walled enclosures, however, have been identified on Carsington pastures, the high ground above the proposed site of Lutudarum. A parallel for the fields in the eastern enclosure survives beside the Romano-British village at Cow Low near Buxton where, as at Roystone, long linear banks parcel up a steep hillside that has not been cultivated since. Long linear fields divided by earthen banks, as on the western face of the east enclosure, also occur at Rainster Rocks, the

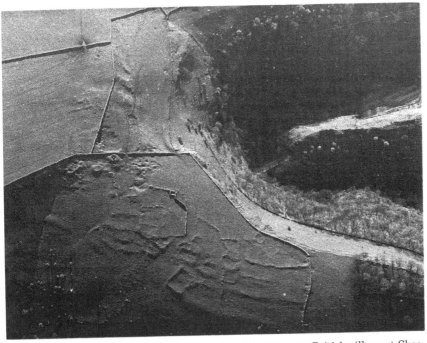

61. Aerial photograph of the earthwork remains of the Romano-British village at Chee Tor (photo: Derrick Riley).

large village and possible market site only 3 kilometres south-east of Roystone.

In common with all the Romano-British settlements in the Peak, Roystone appears to be the product of the Roman need for cash-cropping. The lay-out of the farm reveals that insufficient ground was given over to cultivation. The population of 30-50 people depended instead upon marketing their wool and lead, and obtaining other goods in return. Sufficient hay, oats and perhaps barley could be grown, but other foodstuffs had to be purchased. Yet the density of Roman-period farms in this hitherto deserted region bears witness to the economic boom. Neighbouring farming communities grew up 3 kilometres to the north, west, east, south-east and south of Roystone. Indeed Roman-period communities occur at 3-kilometre intervals along most of the Peakland valleys. Along the flanks of the Manifold Valley is a chain of Romano-British settlements, including the village at Wetton excavated by Samuel Carrington. Between Bakewell and Buxton along the Wye Valley there are just as many settlements, including an exceptionally well-preserved village on Chee Tor.

Despite this expansion, the gritstone areas, including the East Moors, were not colonised as intensively as they had been in the Bronze Age. In contrast to the Bronze Age, large populations probably inhabited the Peak in valley settlements such as Roystone. Whether or not flocks were driven up from the Trent or Don valleys by bands of shepherds during Roman times, as they had been in prehistory, remains unknown. The conspicuous remains of Roman shepherds in caves like those at Dimins Dale near Bakewell or Thor's Cave near Wetton have yet to be interpreted. It is likely, though, that the common pastures were grazed, as they had been in the Bronze Age, by flocks brought from farms like those at Roystone as well as those owned by lowland villa-estates.

During the second and third centuries AD cash-cropping provided the community with a satisfactory livelihood. The imperial market appears to have guaranteed an adequate return on their investment to these farmers for several generations. The few pieces of jewellery as well as the mixture of pottery, only 75 per cent of which comes from the so-called Derbyshire Ware factories near Belper, illustrate that the new generation of Peakland farmers had access to the mass-produced commodities introduced by the Romans. The dwellings excavated at Roystone cannot be dismissed as hovels. In the Midlands the aisled farm, for example, had the status of a proto-villa, while the other farms are of similar proportions to those excavated in the lowlands at Dunston Clump (Nottinghamshire) and Willington in the Trent Valley.

Further testimony to the flourishing economic circumstances in the Peak can be deduced from the aftermath of the revolt of the Brigantes in the 150s. Along with many forts in Brigantian territory, the outpost at Brough-on-Noe in the Hope Valley, which had been abandoned in *c.* 120, was re-garrisoned. This seems to mark the southern limits of the disturbance. Nevertheless, several coin-hoards from the region tend to emphasise that the first generation of Peakland settlers had acquired some wealth and were determined to retain it. The absence of hoards further north in the Pennines shows that the Peak continued to be a distinctive district within the otherwise turbulent Brigantian sphere.

The prosperity of the White Peak farmers seems not to have been harmed by the Brigantian revolt. They were in fact far more vulnerable to changes in the imperial economy, which affected lead exports and the market for wool. Hence, as the third-century recession became increasingly serious in Italy, it was bound to have a highly detrimental effect on marginal economies, especially in far-flung provinces. The recession evidently caused widespread rural poverty and depopulation in Central Italy, and it is hardly surprising to discover much the same in Britain. Thus, after a century and a half, the community at Roystone faced a desperate crisis.

Recession and desertion

The demand for lead must have declined as fewer monumental buildings were constructed following the second-century boom in

Britain, and as the financial recession hit the economy generally. It is possible that direct military control over lead-working came to an end in this period, and thereafter the miners produced rougher pigs that were taken to a collection point such as Carsington but no longer stamped. Some compensation for the slump in demand for lead for building purposes may have come from the new fashion for pewter, which was used to imitate silver tableware. A potentially more serious slump almost certainly affected wool exports. The European trade must have been disrupted by North Sea pirates, by competition from Continental wool exporters, and also by the introduction of new fashions. This will have forced the price of Peakland wool down, compelling the farmers to devote more effort to cultivating crops for subsistence. Meanwhile taxes were being steadily increased by the government as the Empire sought to control its financial predicament. As if all this was not enough, the climate may have gradually deteriorated at about this time.

The archaeology of Britain shows that the third-century recession had a lasting impact upon most areas other than Wessex. Its effects were not immediately cataclysmic, but by the later fourth century even Wessex had been overtaken by the economic malaise. Indeed, before the Roman legions quit the island, the state-run economy had crashed, leaving many parts of the island in aboriginal circumstances.

As far as we can tell from the limited evidence, Roystone, like all farms in the Peak, suffered the consequences of the wider imperial recession. The aisled farmhouse never evolved into a villa; instead it was demolished and replaced by a smaller, rather enigmatic slab-based structure. This seems to have happened to all the buildings at Roystone, and may belong to a new fashion in vernacular architecture favoured in the Peak District as a whole. This change may have occurred for pragmatic reasons. For example, wood was almost certainly no longer as abundant as it had been in the second century, and when old buildings needed to be repaired it may have been necessary to use slabs and turf.

The advent of a shell-tempered type of pottery probably made in Lincolnshire shows that most of the farms had access for a time at least to goods made outside the Peak. The late hearth discovered in house 1 also shows that lead-smelting continued here after the main household in the village had left. The cultivation of the steep slope within the eastern enclosure, where soil movement is very pronounced, reveals that the community had to cultivate the most marginal terrain in order to survive. The tension created by these circumstances may have triggered social unrest, and this could account for the reoccupation of the fort at Brough-on-Noe in the 330s, as well as for a mid-fourth-century coin-hoard from Minninglow. There is no need to look to barbarian invaders as the agents of change. Valleys like

62. Reconstruction of the Roman landscape at Roystone (drawing: Simon Manby).

Roystone were supporting populations that far exceeded their natural carrying capacity, causing increased social conflict and a tendency by many individuals and families to migrate in search of paid work. Doubtless, though, the decline was not constant and unremitting. From time to time the trend of these events may have been mitigated. For instance, the demand for lead to make fashionable pewter tableware may have brought some brief respite from the recession in the Peakland mining industry. But it would be unwise to lay too great an emphasis upon this.

Instead, the constraints of marginality which had had such an impact in the Later Bronze Age, were to prove even more dramatic in the fourth century as the landscape emptied of people almost as swiftly as it had been colonised. The archaeology of Roystone fails to help us chart these final years, so we can only speculate about the course of events. Using villas and villages from the lowlands as a parallel, we can surmise that the smaller farms were gradually abandoned. Some households would have been attracted southwards to occupy land left vacant following depopulation. Others would simply not have 'reproduced' themselves: there was less incentive to have children, and any that there were no doubt eventually migrated to places where work could be found. One or two households probably continued to occupy the valley up to the end of the fourth century, smelting lead and living off small plots and a mixture of stock. Unfortunately, by this time the factories producing the highly distinctive Derbyshire Ware pottery no longer existed, so these final moments of the Peak in Roman

90

A reconstruction of the Romano-British farm

times cannot be detected with any confidence by the archaeologist. Not all memory of Rome had been erased. At Buxton, votive deposits were being made to pagan spirits associated with the spa waters up to about AD 400. Tradition here had outlived reality, for any notion that such places were part of the Empire had long since passed.

*

The Romans provided the incentive to develop the Peak District, as they did in many regions of Britain. They tried, in effect, to extend the champion landscapes established in the later Neolithic to embrace the whole colony. But the trouble with a cash-cropping regime of this kind is that it is extremely vulnerable to change. The written sources tell us that the aristocracy of Rome were gravely dismayed by inflation, high taxation and military expenditure, and forced to desert their country houses in Campania and Etruria. Their plight was in many respects less unfortunate than that of the farmers whose livelihoods had been created by the Roman economic boom. In the uplands of Britain, France, Germany and Spain, farmers like those at Roystone bore the brunt of the crisis.

5

The Making of the Medieval Landscape

Of the new and reformed monastic orders that characterized the opening years of the [twelfth] century, undoubtedly the most influential was the Cistercian. Centrally controlled from the original Burgundian house at Cîteaux, the Cistercians set a uniform standard of austerity very much in harmony with the best instincts of their troubled, but pious, generation. They rejected a missionary role, preferring to inspire rather by example than by precept. They removed themselves, wherever possible, from the world they despaired of. And they sought at each of their many houses to establish a self-sufficient economy, to maintain the flesh though never to indulge it.

Colin Platt, *The Monastic Grange in Medieval England* (1969)

Roystone, according to Professor Cameron, takes its name either from raven's rocks – possibly a reference to the outcrops of dolomitic limestone – or, less probably, from reeve's stones. The word, if it means raven's rocks, may stem from an Anglo-Scandinavian dialect. Whatever the derivation, it is evident that Roystone acquired its name not in Roman times, but either in the Anglo-Scandinavian age or when it became a Cistercian grange – a monastic farm – in the late twelfth century. Unlike the place-name Parwich, which may incorporate the British word *Pebro* – 'the bright one', interpreted as a river – there is no hint of continuity between Roystone's affluent Roman phase and the arrival of the monks from Garendon Abbey. Nevertheless, remote as Roystone was in the twelfth century, it had not been entirely by-passed since the demise of the Romano-British village eight hundred years before.

Anglo-Saxon interlude

Thomas Bateman was no less interested in Anglo-Saxon graves than in prehistoric ones: 'In North Derbyshire the Saxons have generally taken advantage of the Celtic tumuli, and have interred their dead at an inconsiderable depth in them, in the same manner as the North

63. The Benty Grange helmet (courtesy of Sheffield City Museum).

American Indians have done in the ancient mounds in their country ... These are the most modern barrows in this country, as in the sixth century of the Christian era, not very long after the settlement of the Saxons in England, they embraced Christianity ...' In fact, Bateman's discovery of the Peak-dwellers or *Pecsaetan*, as they are called in the seventh-century survey known as the Tribal Hidage, has proved one of the most substantial planks in Anglo-Saxon archaeology. His excavation of the Benty Grange barrow near Arbor Low, for example, revealed a boar's-crested helmet of the kind described in the ninth-century poem *Beowulf*, and ranks alongside the ship burial at Sutton Hoo in Suffolk as one of the major Christian burials from England.

A modern perspective of Anglo-Saxon burial customs in the Peak District has been made possible by John Collis's total excavations of the prehistoric barrow at Wigber Low (see p. 51). This barrow was first explored by John Fossick Lucas, a Victorian antiquary who according to Samuel Carrington – the only person to describe the discovery – unearthed 'some extremely beautiful ornaments partly of gold'. The new excavations show that the ornaments belonged to a group of six or more burials that had been inhumed in and alongside

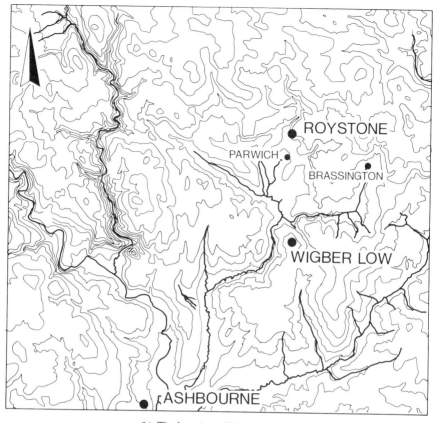

64. The location of Wigber Low.

the ancient mound. Most of the group were buried in graves made within the pre-existing prehistoric cairn, but at least one other was interred in a second cairn overlying a small earlier prehistoric cairn to the south of the main barrow. The pattern of the burials, in other words, maintained the tradition of barrow-burial in the Peak, and was quite as complicated as any in a churchyard. The second barrow at Wigber resembles the Roystone Grange barrow (no. 1) investigated by Bateman in 1849. Here a type 1 enclosure-period wall restricted the antiquarian to an exploration of the secondary barrow. In it he found an inhumation accompanied by a knife. Several archaeologists in recent times have favoured this being an Anglo-Saxon grave belonging to a member of the *Pecsaetan*. If so, it is the only evidence of activity at Roystone between the fourth and tenth centuries. An object like a knife is impossibly difficult to date, so we need to take account of all the other evidence. In our opinion, attractive as Bateman's interpretation might be, it is as likely that the knife is Roman in date and, like the jewellery found in the Lime Kiln barrow excavations nearby,

94

65. Burial 4 at Wigber Low (courtesy of John Collis).

associated with one of the more eminent members of the second-century community at Roystone.

Even so, a sixth-century bronze penannular brooch was found at Pikehall, about three kilometres to the north of Roystone. There had been a Romano-British village at Pikehall beside the Roman road that traverses the White Peak, so perhaps the brooch attests to a community that had outlived the Empire in some form and continued to occupy dwellings and land that had been in use since the second century. The Anglo-Saxon inhumations from Wetton, close to where Samuel Carrington excavated the Romano-British village at Borough Fields (see p. 70), lend support to some continuity of upland settlement in these parts. At Roystone, however, our excavations failed to shed any light on this period, and we were therefore compelled to conclude that the valley was abandoned in Anglo-Saxon times. Shepherds from Anglo-Saxon settlements associated with Ballidon and Parwich may have ventured across to Minninglow and marvelled at the Roman field walls, but for several hundred years, much as we concluded for the later first millennium BC, Roystone was uninhabited.

Until recently we knew nothing more about the Anglo-Saxon history of the area. Then in 1983 a remarkable discovery came to light in a most unexpected place. A seventeenth-century copy of a hitherto unrecorded charter of 963, by which King Edgar granted 5 hides of land at Ballidon to a certain Aethelferth, was found among manuscripts on temporary deposit at Staffordshire Record Office. The copy had certainly once been in the possession of the Staffordshire antiquary John Huntbach (1639-1705) who may have made it from an original obtained when a local abbey sold its library.

The charter takes a well-known form. Essentially it describes a substantial estate that was already a chapelry of the large medieval parish of Bradbourne. (The tenth-century parish was presumably run if not largely owned by the descendants of those buried at Wigber Low.) The chapelry at Ballidon was recognised as a separate civil parish only after 1866, so the charter offers us an unique opportunity to establish its earliest bounds. Professor Nicholas Brooks, in his study of the charter, offers an approximate interpretation of the estate using the brief record of cardinal points of the boundary listed in the document. The description begins at *piowerwic broce*, 'Parwich brook' and aims northwards past the *miclan dic*, 'the big dyke or ditch', to *frigdene*, which Brooks interprets as a point near the present hamlet of Friden. From here the boundary runs to *cyngstraet*, the old Roman road known as The Street. The boundary then follows the road to a point near Ballidon before turning westwards to the starting-point at the Parwich brook. According to Brooks, Ballidon estate in 963 had much the same boundaries as the civil parish of 1866.

This fortuitous discovery shows that Roystone had been in royal

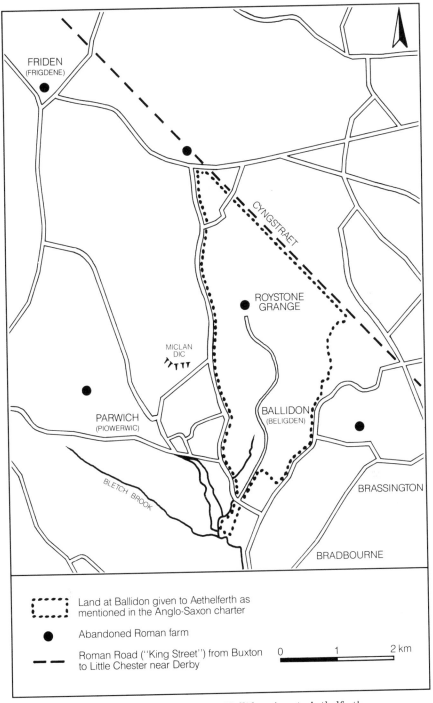

66. The Anglo-Saxon estate at Ballidon given to Aethelferth.

hands within the ninth/tenth-century estate of Bradbourne, and after 963 formed the upland sector of the new Ballidon estate. Like the neighbouring parishes of Brassington and Parwich, Ballidon comprised a cross-section of rolling land at around 180 metres (600 feet) above sea level as well as limestone uplands rising to 340 metres (1,100 feet). As the Anglo-Saxon economy began to flourish at the turn of the millennium, it is likely that Roystone's pastures were grazed regularly by flocks driven up the old Roman track from Ballidon. In 1066, when the estate was in the possession of Leofric and Leofnoth, little had changed. But by 1086 it was in new hands, and as early as this the property at Roystone may have come into the possession of the Herthill family.

The grange at Roystone

Grange place-names abound in the White Peak. Mouldridge Grange, Minninglow Grange, Ballidon Grange and Gotham Grange all lie less than 3 kilometres from Roystone. Some of these are monastic farms, founded in the heady economic expansion of the later twelfth century; some are post-medieval farms that took the name to suggest a long ancestry.

A *grangia* is technically a barn of some kind, but in the twelfth century it became a major feature of the countryside as the monastic orders helped to revive the European economy on a scale that had not been witnessed since Roman times. Granges were monastic farms, founded by monasteries on their property specifically to produce cash-crops for the parent institution to sell. In the Paris Basin, the Loire Valley and Lombardy they were grand farms built in the romanesque style. Professor Colin Platt questions whether English granges were as impressive. Few have been examined, however, and none dating back to the twelfth century has been extensively explored.

In the White Peak the remains of Smerrill Grange near Elton are perhaps the best preserved. Situated overlooking the deep gorge running down to Middleton-by-Youlgreave, Smerrill has the dubious privilege of being the first medieval settlement in the Peak District to be excavated. Thomas Bateman, needless to say, was the excavator, and he was sufficiently uninterested in the results to omit them from his publications. The surviving earthworks suggest that none of the buildings was remotely as grand as the fine French granges of the period. At Roystone a principal aim of our investigation was to chart the history of an upland grange, and to establish what the norm in this region might have looked like.

The earliest known documentary evidence for the existence of Roystone Grange is a reference in the cartulary of Garendon Abbey. Garendon, one of the earliest Cistercian monasteries in England, was

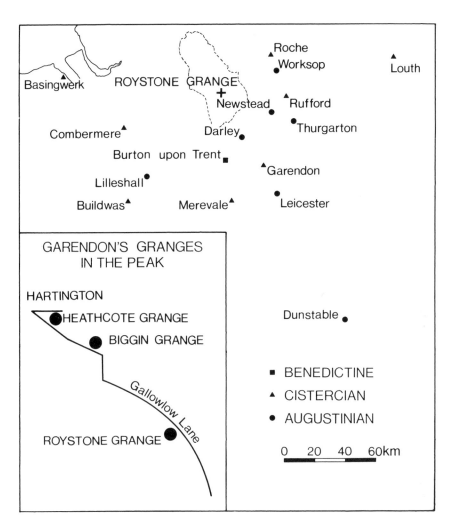

Basingwerk

ROYSTONE GRANGE
+

Roche
Worksop
Louth

Newstead
Rufford

Combermere
Darley
Thurgarton

Burton upon Trent

Garendon

Lilleshall

Buildwas
Merevale
Leicester

GARENDON'S GRANGES
IN THE PEAK

HARTINGTON

HEATHCOTE GRANGE

Dunstable

BIGGIN GRANGE

Gallowlow Lane

ROYSTONE GRANGE

■ BENEDICTINE

▲ CISTERCIAN

● AUGUSTINIAN

0 20 40 60km

67. Location of the Cistercian abbey at Garendon, Leicestershire, and other abbeys in the north Midlands with granges in the White Peak (after Clive Hart).

founded in 1133 in Charnwood Forest, in what is now a suburb of Loughborough. It soon began to acquire property in Leicestershire and then in Derbyshire. On each of its estates it constructed granges and set about vigorously developing its income. By 1225 the abbot had obtained permission to export wool to Flanders and elsewhere on the Continent. In no sense, then, was this a retreat. Quite the contrary, Garendon was a part of a multi-national concern with distinctly capitalist aspirations.

Roystone is called 'Revestones' in the abbey's cartulary, which describes it as a grant to Garendon by Richard de Herthill. It consisted of three acres of land with pasture for three hundred sheep and their

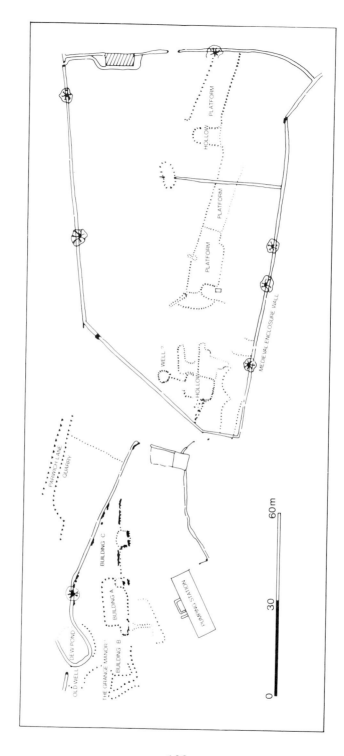

68. Plan of the medieval grange earthworks at Roystone.

OLD WELL

DEW POND

THE GRANGE MANOR

BUILDING B

BUILDING A

BUILDING C

PARWICH LANE

QUARRY

PUMPING STATION

WELL ?

HOLLOW

PLATFORM

PLATFORM

HOLLOW

PLATFORM

MEDIEVAL ENCLOSURE WALL

0   30   60 m

lambs up to the age of one year. A later document contains a confirmation of the grant by Richard's son Adam. This describes not only the place called Revestones and its appurtenances, but also a gift of a cartload of thorns in Ballidon, the right to pasture on Ballidon common, and tenements in the village of Ballidon. The village and the farm were clearly connected, at least as far as the monastery was concerned. A study of the grange's history by Margaret Poulter showed that Richard de Herthill was a late twelfth-century landholder in these parts. We may therefore surmise that Roystone Grange was probably founded in the reign of Henry II or Richard I.

At much the same time Garendon acquired two more estates at Biggin and Heathcote near Hartington. (Gallowlow Lane, running from the north end of Roystone, led directly to these granges (p. 113).) Dunstable Priory, an Augustinian house, meanwhile acquired Mouldridge Grange and other lands in Ballidon, and elsewhere in the White Peak the Abbeys of Combermere, Darley, Leicester, Lilleshall, Merevale, Roche and Rufford acquired lands on which granges were founded.

Revestones was constructed near the only spring in the valley, immediately below a dew-pond that may date from Roman times. This is one of the most sheltered spots in the valley, lying alongside the old Roman track from Ballidon. It is interesting to note, however, that the site of the old Roman village was ignored.

Remains of two house-platforms forming part of the grange were discovered in 1980. In the hot spring of that year the grass was burnt off the east wall of building A, exposing the footings of a substantial building. Sherds found in molehills dotted about the platform showed conclusively that it was medieval in date. Over the next six years the platform was completely uncovered to expose building A. In addition, an even more impressive building (B) was discovered immediately south of A, and a third (C) was identified immediately north of A. The history of this chain of buildings, running B-A-C from south to north, is complicated. But it merits telling because it is probably fairly typical of most of the granges founded by monasteries as sheep ranches on the White Peak.

The archaeological sequence

Phase 1

In the late twelfth or early thirteenth century a terrace revetted by dolomite boulders was created a short distance downhill of the Roman-period dew-pond. At the back of the terrace a bank at least a metre across, again revetted by boulders, separated it from the pond itself. Building A was constructed upon this terrace. Its walls remain

69. Grange building A, looking north (scale = 2 m) (photo: Richard Hodges).

an enigma: no post-holes were found, while other phase 1 walls discovered in the excavations suggest that simple drystone walls made of local carboniferous limestone were the norm.

Little trace of the inner layout of the building has survived. Only two rows of finely cut stylobate post-pads suggest that building A at this time was an aisled construction resembling, for example, the Romano-British manor at Roystone and the twelfth-century woolhouse at Fountains Abbey. Revestones, it seems, was divided into three bays. The south bay contained a hooded fireplace, judging by the scatter of small nails around a surviving hearth. (The fire itself was made upon a worn sandstone quern.) The central bay was dominated by a deep hollow that was eventually filled in with packed rubble. The north bay was flagged with limestone paving bisected by a simple drain running downslope from west to east.

South of building A and pre-dating building B traces of several structures were discovered. Close to the south wall of building A was a deep and sharply defined pit (feature 310) within which were two substantial post-holes. Next to this a tank was discovered, served by a simple drain cut into the natural clay. The walls of the tank were made of drystone bonded together with a bright yellow heavy clay. Remains of a drain arced away downslope, and one fragment beneath the later building B was especially well-preserved. Both tanks may have been associated with the production of wool.

It is tempting to assume that building C, the northernmost of the

70. Grange building B, looking west, with building A (*top right*) (scale = 2 m) (photo: Richard Hodges).

trio of structures, also existed at this time. It sat on a well-defined terrace of the kind constructed to accommodate building A, which awaits excavation at some future date. Even so, several features can be made out on the terrace. These suggest that a building of some sort occupied its southern half separated by a hollow from a simple trapezoidal-shaped yard or pen at the northern end.

Phase 2

This phase was notable for the construction of building B, a structure more typical of a monastery than an upland farm. It probably dates to the early thirteenth century.

Building B was constructed at right-angles to building A, running down the slope, presumably in a bid to accommodate two floors in its eastern half. The rectangular building was 13.5 metres long and 6 metres wide with two rooms divided by an inner wall; its walls had been constructed on a plinth about 80 cm wide. The masons carefully selected the stone and trimmed the pieces to shape as they erected the walls, leaving chippings alongside. A stairway, of which two stone steps survived, linked the western, upper room to the ground floor eastern room. The surviving foundations of a small room or annexe on the south side suggest that there was probably an external staircase providing access to the first floor. A drain was built alongside the south wall, while a similar drain starting on the west side of building A led around and alongside the north wall of the new building.

103

The finely cut stones of the ashlar doorway along with the quoining leave no doubt that this was an elegant hall, quite unlike the phase 1 building A. Much of building B has gone, but sufficient survives to offer a clue to its appearance. We can compare it with similar buildings surviving to this day at Lincoln (the Jew's House), Norwich (the Music House) and Southampton (Canute's Palace), and the East and West Guesthouses at Fountains Abbey which were designed on the same scale. Not far from Garendon Abbey itself, at Donington le Heath (Leicestershire) an elegant manor house, erected in this period, still stands. Unlike these other halls, though, an absence of tiles associated with building B at Roystone indicates that it was roofed with either thatch or shingles.

Quite what happened to the original building A when the new one was built is a matter for conjecture, but in our opinion it is most likely that buildings A and C remained largely unaltered in this phase. It was at about this time, though, that the bank separating the west (back) wall of building A from the old Roman dew-pond was reinforced with a fine drystone wall. Much of the earth required for this bank was probably found when building B was constructed.

Phase 3

Building B was used for only a very short time. In all likelihood the ground floor was repeatedly flooded by water pouring down the slope from the spring beside the dew-pond. Indeed, as the earlier tank on this spot shows, the site was a natural reservoir for water. As a result it appears that the southern half of the elegant new hall was demolished and much of the stone used to rebuild the bow-shaped walls of the aisled building A. In addition, it seems that the southern half of building B was made into a rough-surfaced yard. The steps which had once served the different floors within the old hall now led from the yard through a porch to the north door (in fact part of building B) of the aisled hall. This doorway was now linked by a short corridor to building A. All in all, some inventive botching went on to make use of the existing walls.

Building A was substantially altered too. Its floor level was raised rather as in the Romano-British farm. A small oven was created in the south bay, and a central fireplace was situated where the earlier through-passage had been in earlier times, while the flagged north end survived. A wide north door continued to provide access to building C, but a new door in the centre of the east wall lead directly to the central fireplace. A small annexe was tucked between building A and all that remained of building B to the north of the improvised corridor.

This arrangement, however, spanned a brief period only, and by the later thirteenth century it appears that the entire complex was

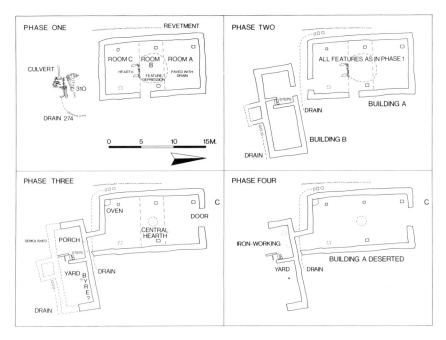

71. Four medieval phases of grange buildings A & B.

deserted. But the site was not to be permanently abandoned. David Twigge's father, who remembered Roystone from his boyhood at the turn of the century, insisted that we were digging in the wrong place. Only a sheep-pen, he said, would be found here! He wasn't exactly proved right, but he wasn't entirely wrong either!

Phase 4

Soon after the abandonment of the site during the fourteenth and fifteenth centuries, the upper room within building B (which had become a porch in phase 3) was used for some light iron-smelting. In the lower room remains of a post-pad (to support a timber upright) suggest it was now made over to some temporary use, perhaps as a dairy or stable. To the south of it a small type 3 field wall was found, overlying the largely robbed remains of the hall. It seems likely that building A continued to be used as a barn of some sort. Large numbers of sheep's teeth show that flocks made use of it from time to time before it fell down.

Phase 5

The entire area was abandoned, the buildings thoroughly robbed of their good stone, and a layer of stones covered the site.

Phase 6

Among the recent activities detected during the excavations was the burial of a horse into the centre of building B. The horse was accompanied by a small bell and a stoneware pitcher. After careful excavation and a good deal of debate about the possible ritual aspects of this unlikely discovery, Charles Etches, who was born at Roystone in 1918 (see p. 147) informed us that the animal (called Polly) was buried in 1928!

Revestones

The outline history of this building does not do it justice. A building is far more than its walls and fireplaces. The first farm here seems to have been a vernacular barn-like hall resembling the Roman-period manor. It had a living-room, a cross-passage and a small dairy. North of it building C was probably a small cattle-shed with a yard attached to it. Then, we may assume, someone from Garendon decided that a grander dwelling was needed, and called for an architect to put up a fine hall with ashlar quoins and a skilfully chamfered doorstep. This building would not have looked out of place on a French grange. Presumably the ground floor was used for storage, while the first floor served as a reception room and chambers for the granger who managed the estate.

Unfortunately, the architect drew up his plan in the summer – presumably one of the last of the exceptionally warm summers between the tenth and later twelfth centuries. For as the thirteenth century drew on, the climate deteriorated and this hillside, to judge from our experiences, turned into a quagmire as water spilled over from the spring a little higher up the slope. The drains around building B failed to keep the water out, and as a result the ground floor was regularly flooded. This must have damaged the building beyond repair, necessitating its partial demolition. The inventive botching of phase 3 involved restoring the original hall and using part of the grand single-phase building B as a porch to cover those entering from the south. Porches like this became a necessary feature of Pennine farms in the later Middle Ages as the Little Ice Age set in. Even so, there continued to be a problem with water spilling across the site in winter. A cess-pit cut at the back of building A, for instance, must have been full of water for much of the year. Building A was certainly a little grander now. The cross-passage had been removed and a larger reception room with a central hearth occupied two bays of the building. The old dairy may have become a pantry, with the milking taking place in building C.

By 1300 if not earlier the conditions here must have been pretty unpleasant, and it seems that the site was deserted in favour of a drier

72. A thirteenth-century green-glazed jug from building A (courtesy of Sheffield City Museum).

spot in the fields to the north. Here the earthworks of the farm spanning the period from c. 1300 to c. 1750 can be still seen. The old buildings were not forgotten, however, and they were used for a while before bits were taken for other purposes. Part of the ashlar lintel of building B, for example, can be seen in the east door in the south face of the great barn in the present farm.

We have probably excavated only a small part of Revestones. Traces were found of a possible building to the south of building B, and adjacent to building C, but separated by a Roman-period wall, lies a garden that belonged to the grange (see below). Other buildings almost certainly lay dotted around a yard situated below the terrace, and we might thus envisage the lane from Ballidon leading into a yard overlooked by the farmhouse. Later, when the site was deserted, the lane by-passed the complex, as it does now, and headed directly to the new site of the grange.

An impression of the variety of buildings in a normal grange was recorded by Fountains Abbey for their farm at Aldburgh. The inventory describes the buildings as set in an enclosed court, including a dwelling-house for the farmer, a fulling-mill, a messuage* called 'kynhouse', another messuage called 'smythshous', some stables, a

*A house with adjoining land.

cottage called 'colhouse', a house called 'kylnhous' and another known as 'waynmanhouse'; next to the gate was another cottage known as 'couhowplace'. The domestic quarters are recorded for several granges of this period. At Wharram in Yorkshire, for example, the abbot's chamber was adjoined by a hall and a cellar. Beds, chests and chairs are listed in the chambers; cupboards, trestle-tables, benches and forms in the halls; pots, pans, spits and firedogs in the kitchens.

Few traces of these furnishings have survived at Roystone. We are better informed about the diet and culinary activities of the household. The animal bones, for instance, tell us what was eaten here in the thirteenth century. About 60 per cent of the bones were those of sheep, with only 7 per cent being cattle bones and 2 per cent pig. Cattle, because of their size, would have provided a slightly larger proportion of the meat consumed by the household. Of the sheep bones, medium ribs seem to be the most common, indicating that there was a preference for chops! The bones of a horse, rabbits, geese, chicken, at least one fish, and a red deer were also represented in the sample. Evidently the farmers at Roystone did not experience a harsh regime as far as food was concerned.

This picture of life on the grange is supported by other finds from the excavations. The potsherds include a surprising number of fine glazed jugs made in the pottery-making centres at Birley Hill (near Derby), Brackenfield (near Clay Cross) and Chesterfield. These were presumably bought in the local markets at Ashbourne or Hartington. Coarse pots are rare. There are fragments of distinctive shell-tempered dairy pans made in Lincolnshire, but very few cooking-pots such as are found in peasant communities. This may be because they had bronze cooking and serving dishes, as is known to have been the case in most monasteries. The pottery finds, however, are overshadowed by the discovery of an unprepossessing fragment of an early-thirteenth-century urinal made of thin, pale yellow glass. Glass urinals are extremely rare in England at this time, and this find emphasises that some members of the grange household aspired to a grand style of living. The metalwork also endorses this view. Besides practical tools like knives, a chisel and a pair of woollen shears, several fine gilded buckles and catches for elegant boxes were found. In addition, a fragment of a sixth-century square-headed brooch with gold gilding, and a delicately enamelled roundel that had once been attached to a seventh-century hanging bowl were found on the site. Could these have been found by early Cistercian antiquarians, either locally, or near Garendon in Leicestershire?

By all accounts the Cistercians were an austere order. Yet the material culture of Roystone is quite at odds with this ethic. By any peasant standards, the brethren working the farm lived extremely well. This is not really so surprising. Garendon Abbey itself earned a

73. Seventh-century enamelled roundel (an escutcheon from a bronze hanging bowl) found in grange building B (courtesy of Sheffield City Museum).

rather dubious reputation for good living – particularly heavy beer-drinking. On more than one occasion its abbot and his brethren were reprimanded. It is in fact unlikely that many monks ever worked at Roystone. Instead lay brethren would have been recruited to run the farm. As a rule a granger or grange master was hired to oversee the estate. He was answerable to the cellarer at the monastery, but it was up to him to find servants for the grange, staff for the workshops, ploughmen and shepherds. Some were hired as lay brethren, while others were tied peasants released for certain periods of the year from the manors on which they served. On an estate of this size, there would have been a group of between ten and twenty brethren. The granger would have kept the accounts, and with three or four brethren as assistants, he would have represented the authority and discipline of the mother-house. He, for instance, would have led the staff in the daily routine of prayer. Most of the workforce was probably drawn from Ballidon, the nearest village, contravening for practical reasons – as all Cistercian granges did – the ideals of isolation laid down in the order's Rule. By depopulating neighbouring villages for their own financial ends, the Cistercians gained a reputation as single-minded profiteers. One thirteenth-century archbishop of Canterbury described them as the 'hardest neighbours that a priest or layman could have'. Yet for those fortunate enough to live on the estate there were obvious material advantages that must have weighed with many Peakland families as they despatched their sons to work on these upland farms.

The grange estate

In Chapter 2 we described the single-orthostat boulder walls of the medieval period. These type 3 walls mostly survive as foundations

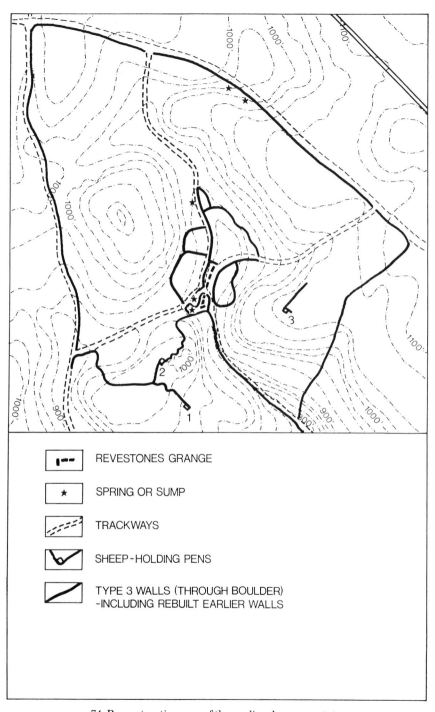

REVESTONES GRANGE

SPRING OR SUMP

TRACKWAYS

SHEEP-HOLDING PENS

TYPE 3 WALLS (THROUGH BOULDER)
-INCLUDING REBUILT EARLIER WALLS

74. Reconstruction map of the medieval grange estate.

110

75. Medieval sheep-pen 2 (photo: Richard Hodges).

beneath later rebuilds, but in some cases stretches of complete walling can still be seen. The survival of these walls allows us to reconstruct the extent and lay-out of the grange farm.

The estate appears to have covered about 400 acres (150 ha), and lay either side of Roystone valley. The grange itself lies close to the southern boundary which from here follows a wriggling line around the hill across to the Parwich-Pikehall road. From this point the boundary heads north alongside the Parwich-Pikehall road as far as Gallowlow Lane. It then turns eastwards and follows Gallowlow Lane for more than 2 kilometres to a point on the top close to Minninglow whence a direct line could be drawn to the south wall of the old Roman east enclosure. The final section of the boundary then follows the line of the Roman wall.

Within the estate lay several fields and at least two driving walls leading up to sheep-pens. A large field in which traces of ridge-and-furrow ploughing can be seen lies on the west-facing slope overlooking the grange. A small walled garden divided into two by a low bank lies adjacent to the grange complex. Test-pits in this area revealed a rich black soil, several sherds of green glazed jugs, and a horse burial which, as we have seen, dated to 1928! Four other walled paddocks were made in the valley, one of which made use of a stretch of old Roman wall. The lay-out of the fields suggests that this was a sheep ranch with almost no capacity for growing crops. Most of the estate was for infield grazing, with paddocks near the grange designed to control stock. One or two of these paddocks may also have been used for cattle. In summer the flocks were probably taken onto the commons beyond

111

76. Gallowlow Lane, running along the northern boundary of the grange estate (looking north) (photo: Ray Manley).

the estate, as was permitted by the grant made to Garendon Abbey.

Further evidence of the outfield grazing is to be found in the disposition of the sheep-pens. Two pens made of single orthostats lie on the hill south-west of the grange outside the estate. Both pens are divided into two compartments by stone partitions. Pen 2 is exceptionally well-preserved, but pen 1 is perhaps the most interesting. A long well-preserved driving wall, branching off from the estate boundary, wriggles its way about 200 metres to the pen, suggesting that, like the type 4 double-orthostat walls of Roman times, this was built through woodland or recently cleared undergrowth. Pen 1 and its wall may have been used until Victorian times when a field barn was built to one side of the pen. A third pen (no. 3) and a short stretch of driving wall lay within the estate on the hilltop close to the Lime Kiln barrow.

The boundaries of the estate may have been defined by pre-existing features, though this is open to debate. The valley fields, for instance, lie either side of the lane that runs from Ballidon up through Roystone to Gallowlow Lane. The estate was traversed on its south side by a lane from Parwich which can be traced almost to Gallowlow Lane heading for Minninglow. At the point where this lane passed through the western enclosure of the old Romano-British farm, a deep holloway

112

began to form. The holloway is quite visible today, and indicates that this stretch of Roman walling was maintained in medieval times. Either the northern and eastern sides of the estate follow Gallowlow Lane, or the lane followed the bounds of the estate. It is a chicken-and-egg debate as to which came first. There is no record of the lane before 1620, and it seems likely that if it had existed in the tenth century it might have been mentioned when the Ballidon estate was given away by King Edgar. The lane leads from Brassington to Hartington and appears to serve sheep ranches in the White Peak, like Roystone, which used the market founded at Hartington in 1200. It was certainly the quickest route between Garendon's three Peakland granges at Biggin, Heathcote and Roystone.

In contrast to many lowland estates where some continuity of Roman and Anglo-Saxon boundaries has been shown, at Roystone there is little overlap in the lay-out of the Roman and medieval farms. The Romano-British farm was designed to serve a village principally concerned with running sheep. The medieval farm was essentially a sheep ranch, a highly specialised business supported by the parent abbey at Garendon as far as subsistence products were concerned. The farm buildings themselves, as on so many granges, were located where it made good sense. Hence at Roystone the farm was placed beside the main water supply. The climatic optimum of the twelfth century, when summers were appreciably warmer than they are now, may have necessitated choosing this site. The old Roman dew-pond, at the north end of the second-century village, had almost certainly dried up and disappeared. The farm was located close to the ragged western stretch of the south boundary of the estate, defined, we might speculate, after negotiation with landowners and shepherds from Ballidon and Parwich who must also have used the adjacent common ground. By contrast, when defining the eastern half of the south boundary the granger doubtless made use of the extant Roman enclosure wall, bisecting the pasture on Ballidon Moor.

Ballidon 'in the valley shaped like a sack'

Roystone probably drew its labour from Ballidon, the nearest village. Moreover, it is doubtful that there was ever a chapel at Roystone, so the lay brethren must have walked down the lane to pray at the now much-restored Norman church. Today the church stands isolated in the fields, marking the medieval extent of the presently much reduced village. The remains of the medieval village can be clearly made out in the fields beside the church. The grassy humps and bumps when seen from the air form a row of farms beside lanes leading away to Bradbourne and Parwich. And running out from the earthworks are the remains of medieval furlongs, looking today like an undulating sea

77. The shrunken medieval village at Ballidon from the air. Note the Norman church (*centre*) separated by earthworks from the modern hamlet (photo: Derrick Riley).

of ridge and furrow. The archaeology of Ballidon therefore provides a fine example of a Peakland medieval village to compare with the adjacent Cistercian estate at Roystone.

In 1986 the construction of a silage pit within the medieval settlement provided an opportunity for a small excavation. The results were hardly remarkable, though the sequence of activity on the site was intriguing. The earliest traces found were of a Roman-period pond. Whether a Romano-British village was located nearby remains to be seen, but it is such a good spot that it would be surprising if a farm, at least, had not taken advantage of the meadows in the lee of the limestone scarp. By Domesday, as we have seen, there was a flourishing village, named, according to Professor Cameron, after 'the valley shaped like a sack'. The excavation here revealed little in the way of structures, but was helpful as far as dating the earthworks is concerned. A few sherds of eleventh/twelfth-century pottery, and many sherds like those from Roystone were found in the trench. But the greater part of the assemblage belongs to the late Middle Ages. A census of 1563 shows that at that time there were about 16 households (approximately 80 people) in the settlement with 1,910 acres of ground (i.e. on average each household possessed about 119 acres, or one-quarter of the land farmed at Roystone). In 1563 Parwich, a comparatively large village, boasted 30 households (approximately 150

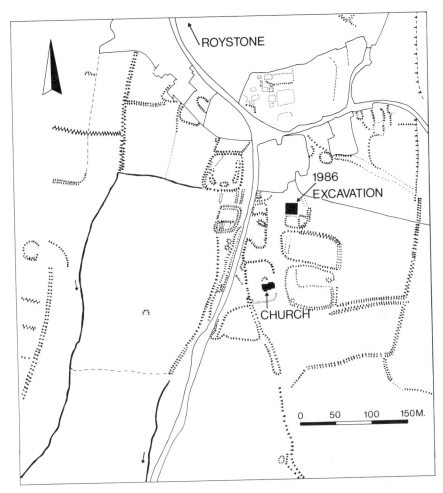

78. Plan of the shrunken village at Ballidon showing the location of the 1986 excavations.

people), and Ashbourne, the nearest market town, had a total population of between 600 and 650.

Medieval Ballidon lay either side of a lane running up to Roystone. Cow Close Farm, a fine eighteenth-century building, almost certainly marks the site of a late medieval farm alongside this lane, which in turn probably overlies the levelled remains of a Late Saxon building. It is likely that a line of other farms at Ballidon were abandoned in the late Middle Ages and remain today in the form of earthworks. As Fig. 78 reveals, each farm lay within a rectangular yard. Many of the yards were probably sub-divided, and in one part in most cases the low relief of a house platform can be made out. Excavations of a similar deserted site at Barton Blount in south Derbyshire showed that in the later

115

Middle Ages, as the winter weather deteriorated during the early years of the Little Ice Age, cattle tended increasingly to be kept in the yards, whose perimeter walls became boldly accentuated in contrast to the other features. The yards not only ensured that the cattle were well cared for, but also prevented the beasts from unnecessarily poaching the ground. (In winter today dairy cattle roam around Ballidon making deep tracks and mires that scar the ancient landscape.)

The cultivated infield seems to consist of two distinct parts. On the slope behind the church a prominent bank, bisected at one point by a holloway, separates the strip fields at the back of the farms from those lying further up the slope. Traces of a similar bank lie on the western side of the village, alongside Ballidon brook. In fact, in both cases these banks are headlands – lines left unploughed when the plough-teams turned at the end of the strips. At some stage there may have been a hedge on top of this bank, making it a good deal less conspicuous than it is today.

The archaeology of Ballidon helps to shed a little light on the medieval character of better-known villages in the White Peak. For instance, the present villages of Chelmorton and Sheldon have attracted a lot of attention from geographers and historians who have interpreted their narrow walled fields as indications of the pattern of medieval strip cultivation. The prominent banks or 'town rings' surrounding these villages have also caught the imagination of many scholars, who have envisaged these as enclosures fencing in the community and its cultivated furlongs while keeping out the stock and intruders. The spectacular pattern of walled strips at Chelmorton, in particular, has led to much speculation that the villagers practised a mixed agrarian regime best known in the lowlands of the Midlands. All of this seems highly improbable. First, as we have seen, the eighteenth-century enclosure walls may be most misleading, offering an impression and no more of late medieval circumstances, and giving us little clue, for example, about the later twelfth-century field arrangements. Secondly, as Chelmorton and Sheldon are well over 300 metres (1000 feet) above sea level, several hundred feet higher than Ballidon, they would have been very sensitive to microclimatic changes, let alone the end of the high medieval climatic optimum in the thirteenth century and the onset of the Little Ice Age. Whether it was possible to cultivate cereals at this height after *c.* 1200 remains to be examined critically. Certainly the well-preserved remains of four granges near Chelmorton in the Dove Valley (Cotesfield Grange owned by Combermere Abbey; Cronkston, Needham and Pilsbury Granges owned by Merevale Abbey) show that, as at Roystone, very little ground was given over to arable cultivation. Admittedly these granges were almost certainly sheep ranches like Roystone, and so not suitable comparisons with which to interpret the medieval economy of the

79. Aerial photograph of Chelmorton and its strip fields (photo: Ray Manley).

80. Aerial photograph of Haddon Hall (*top left*), an Elizabethan house, and the earthworks of the medieval village that it replaced (*right*) (photo: Derrick Riley).

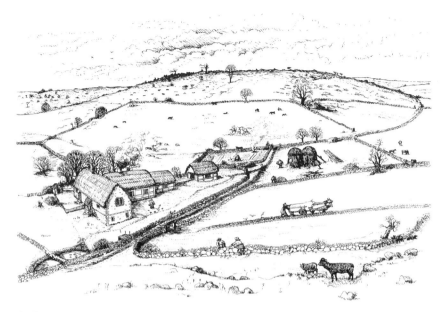

81. Reconstruction of the grange and its landscape at Roystone (drawing: Simon Manby).

White Peak villages. It is quite possible, as in the contrasting cases of Roystone and Ballidon, that these granges and Chelmorton might have practised very different agrarian cycles. Further fieldwork is urgently needed if we are to appreciate how White Peak villagers fared through the ups and downs of the Middle Ages and, by implication, what conditions were like on the Derbyshire Dome for peasants in Roman and prehistoric times.

From grange to hill-farm

Granges like Roystone, directed by lay brethren and worked by a dependent peasantry, were, according to Professor R.A. Donkin, 'the most important single contribution of the new monastic orders, and particularly of the Cistercians, to the landscape and economy of the twelfth and thirteenth centuries'. But the expanding European market that had stimulated large-scale agricultural organisation began to show signs of contraction during the thirteenth century. By the fourteenth century, even before the Black Death decimated the population, England's rural economy was in decline. Recession and political instability, aggravated by the onset of the Little Ice Age and the perniciousness of the plagues and ensuing famines, caused most religious houses to make an urgent reappraisal of their assets. Like modern multi-national companies, they began to reorganise their investments. Upland granges, far from the boardrooms in lowland monasteries, were bound to suffer. At meetings in chapter-houses all over England, the decision was made to lease the granges to lay tenants, thereby shifting the risk to the independent farmer.

As early as the mid-thirteenth century the Cistercians in Britain were finding it difficult to sustain their finances. Mounting rural prosperity had begun to undermine recruitment into the order. At Garendon Abbey, much-publicised self-indulgence by successive abbots and their lay brethren gained them an unfortunate reputation. By the later thirteenth century Garendon was leasing out its granges in Leicestershire and doubtless had already begun this process in the Peak.

It is not difficult to imagine the implications of this drastic turn of events. A farming family was now offered the opportunity to replace the granger and his staff. Of course, the monastery would have taken a good rent, hoping that the farmer could maintain or even improve upon the stocking levels. But apart from the wider malaise of the age, the farmer and his family were bound to be affected by some obvious practical difficulties. The buildings of the grange itself were designed for lay brethren and unsuited to the new occupants. Many buildings, Professor Platt suggests, may have been used for storage purposes. The monastery was no longer prepared to maintain, repair or alter the grange; this was now the problem of the farmer. 'In these circumstances', Professor Platt concludes, 'there could have been nothing unusual in the total destruction of many grange buildings even before the dissolution of the monasteries.'

It may be no coincidence that Richard de Herthill's original grant to Garendon Abbey was confirmed in the reign of Henry III (1216-1272) and again in 1340. It may have been in this period that Roystone was leased to a lay tenant. It is possible that the Cokaine family, who inherited the manor of Ballidon from the Herthill family by marriage in the late fourteenth century, leased back the grange at Roystone as part of the consolidation of their lands. However, the earliest reference to the leasing of the grange by the abbey is in a letter from the Abbot of Garendon to Thomas Cromwell, Henry VIII's minister, dated 15 March 1535/6. The reference is in answer to a letter from Cromwell brought to Garendon by one Francis Basset in which the latter asks for a new lease for the grange called 'Rewestones'. In his efforts to explain why he cannot accede to this request the abbot states that the grange was let to one Rowland Babyngton eight years before. It seems that William Basset had leased the grange, presumably as a tenant of Babyngton, but died within the term. Henry Cokyn of Ballidon apparently married the widow of William Basset and occupied the grange. Just to complicate this story, Cokyn failed to keep up his rent-payments, possibly because he was compelled by his wife to keep his step-son, Francis Basset, at an expensive school. As a result the

82. Aerial photograph showing the location of the grange and the field in which the late medieval and early modern farm was situated (photo: Derrick Riley).

abbey repossessed the grange, but on the eve of the Dissolution of the Monasteries allowed Henry Cokyn to return for the remaining two years of his lease.

The desertion of building A at the end of phase 3 may well have been brought about by the reorganisation of the estate in the late thirteenth century. Much as Platt describes for Yorkshire granges at this time, the old buildings at Roystone were turned into makeshift barns and workshops. It is not hard to imagine the new farmer and his wife being pretty dismissive about the old grange, especially if they first arrived during the winter. Its dark, dank position as the winters became harsher would not have been at all attractive. A new farmhouse in the meadow to the north would have been lighter and drier. It was here, we propose, that William Basset lived.

Little change was made to the estate. There is no evidence of new fields or increased cultivation. Traces of metal-working in the old buildings are no more than a hint that local veins of iron and lead were beginning to be explored once more. Even if the new owners of Roystone sought to supplement their incomes in this way, it is worth bearing in mind that the 400-acre farm was approximately four times the size of the average farm at Ballidon and Parwich (see p. 114). With the rebuilding of the English wool industry in the fifteenth and sixteenth centuries, it stood to benefit handsomely. Indeed, we must not overlook the fact that Henry Cokyn not only wished but also could afford to send Francis Basset to school. Thus, unlike the manorial family of Roman times who were ultimately crushed by the third-century economic recession, the survival of the farm at Roystone through the fourteenth century and its steady success thereafter is a good illustration of the new tenacious social order in England. With doughty resolution, in common with yeomen all over England, Peakland farmers in this age laid the foundations for Britain's mighty economic expansion in the eighteenth century. Unlike their Bronze Age and Roman forebears, the late medieval hill-farmers turned marginality to their advantage, avoiding extinction as the European economy passed through yet another recession.

6

Towards the Wealth of the Nation

> The capital employed in agriculture not only puts into motion a greater quantity of productive labour than any capital employed in manufactures, but in proportion, too, to the quantity of productive labour which it employs it adds a much greater value to the annual produce of the land and labour of the country, to the real wealth and revenue of its inhabitants. Of all the ways in which a capital can be employed, it is by far the most advantageous to the society.
>
> Adam Smith, *An Inquiry into the Nature and Causes of the Wealth of Nations* (1776)

In Adam Smith's judgment the Industrial Revolution was based on the sound development of agricultural practice in Britain. Industry and agriculture went hand-in-hand to provide the conditions for Britain's emergence as the most powerful country in the world. In most surveys of post-medieval agriculture the history of hill-farming features only modestly. An unwritten assumption exists that once agricultural intensification gathered momentum, hill-farms were left behind, remote and marginal. The history of Roystone, like that of most Peakland farms, largely confounds this commonly-held view. The landscape is indelibly imprinted with the evidence of near-continuous changes implemented by generations of farmers who, building on the foundations laid by their medieval predecessors, were keeping pace with the rapid advancement of the whole country.

As early as the sixteenth century the English economy, in common with that of most Continental countries, experienced a revival which gave rise to a rapid growth in the population. These circumstances had their own knock-on effect: prices, for example, increased fivefold between 1530 and 1640, and as a result, farming became increasingly profitable. From this time significant improvements were made in the quality of stock. First sheep, then cattle and horses were carefully bred to produce new ideal forms, one of which is eulogised in 'The Derbyshire Ram', a popular folk song of this era. From the late sixteenth century farmers were also encouraged to use the land more productively by sub-dividing their largest fields. Inevitably, too, there were substantial profits to be made from enclosing the common lands,

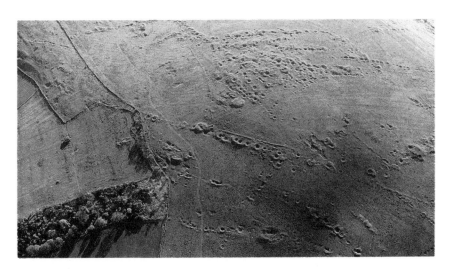

83. Aerial photograph of lead rakes near Carsington (photo: Derrick Riley).

traditionally used by all members of rural society. Resistance to enclosure in many parts was ferocious, but the big landowners tended to win the day. Derbyshire, as we shall see, was no exception.

After the first phase of enclosure came the steady development of rural industries. In Derbyshire this involved lead and copper-mining, and then the construction of the milling industry. At the end of the seventeenth century Derbyshire lead was quarried out of long trenches that followed the lead rakes, much as in Roman times. But the invention of new drainage technology, and the introduction in 1715 of a steam engine at Yatestoop mine at Winster, only three years after the first ever Newcomen engine had been commissioned at a Midlands coalpit, made it possible to explore deeply buried veins for the first time. There followed an explosion of activity which has left the White Peak covered in scars. A little later, Richard Arkwright's successful application of water power for textile processing in 1771 profoundly altered the Derwent and Wye valleys, along which numerous mills sprang up. Like the Derbys of Coalbrookdale, Arkwright set in motion changes that would alter the face of Britain.

Industry and agriculture were an inseparable partnership. The second wave of enclosures, this time confirmed by Acts of Parliament, finally removed the last expanses of common ground in England. The agronomist Robert Bakewell (1725-1795) calculated that 'fifty acres of pasture divided into five enclosures will go as far as in grazing cattle as sixty acres all in one piece'. Enclosure in the later eighteenth century was transacted upon a stupendous scale, and was quite as impressive in its vision as the industrial achievements of men like Richard Arkwright. Needless to say, it aroused passionate opposition. John Clare, the East Anglian poet, put his feelings into verse:

6. Towards the Wealth of the Nation

Inclosure, thou'rt a curse upon the land
And tasteless was the wretch who thy existence plann'd.

In the wake of enclosure came the railway. The Cromford and High Peak Railway was approved by Act of Parliament in 1825. In many ways it was an upland version, at least in the minds of its builders, of the Cromford canal, forging a link between it and the Peak Forest canal at Whaley Bridge. Josias Jessop, the engineer, was the son of the builder of the Cromford canal. The route involved excavating deep cuttings, and then as it wound around Minninglow Hill, overlooking Roystone, making embankments of the kind William Ruskin described as 'vaster than the walls of Babylon'. So steep was the incline up onto the White Peak plateau that horses were needed to draw the engines. By 1841, however, the horse teams had been replaced by locomotives, and fourteen years later passengers could take this slow scenic trip.

The railway destroyed the diversity and isolation of the English landscape. Above all, laments W.G. Hoskins, it hastened the end of the regional building styles which had been such an important feature of the landscape. It also opened up the hills to the same massive exploitation industrial expansion had introduced to the valleys. Quarries for building-stone and sand-pits for the bricks required as town-housing needs exploded in mid-Victorian times both damaged the landscape beyond repair. None of these developments by-passed Roystone, where the landscape – unaffected by the Armada, the Civil War, the Restoration, the loss of America, or the Napoleonic Wars – bears witness to many changes. The activities imprinted on these hills, like those on almost every English farm, cumulatively attest to the making and in many ways the triumph of modern Britain.

Genesis of a hill-farm

For several years after the Dissolution of the Monasteries in 1544 Roystone was held by Rowland Babyngton, together with several other places including Mouldridge Grange at Pikehall (3 kilometres north of Roystone). Then, as we have seen, the farm reverted to the tenure of William Basset. As Basset was long since dead his son Francis must be meant here unless he had another son. After this the history of the grange is somewhat confused. It is next mentioned in 1599 when Sir Humphrey Ferrers brought a complaint against Sir Anthony Ashley, Philip Okeover and Francis Cokayne, claiming that through enclosure and other means they had impeded his and his tenants' rights to pasture sheep and other animals on the common pasture in Ballidon and on Ballidon Moor. The law suit was still unresolved in 1612 and had delayed the enclosure of Ballidon Moor. In the meantime in 1609, by Letters Patent of James I, Roystone had passed to John Shepherd of

84. Dry-stone embankment on the Cromford and High peak railway near Minninglow (photo: Ray Manley).

Wimbourne St Giles, a yeoman and nominee of Sir Anthony Ashley. The farm changed hands twice more in almost as many years as the enclosure dispute dragged on, and eventually was held by Richard Kinge for a yearly rent of 10s. Roystone then passes out of sight. Tithes were not paid on the grange because the Cistercians had been exempted. By the late eighteenth century it was the property of Thomas Taylor and through him passed to William Webster, who owned the property at the time of the Title Commissioners' Survey in 1843.

From the fourteenth century onwards the farm almost certainly lay in the valley-bottom, 200 metres north of its twelfth-century site. Here the distinctive outline of at least two large revetted platforms can be seen and, less clearly, an associated cluster of small earthworks. The Ballidon lane passed in front of the buildings beside the eastern wall of the field. It almost certainly continued on to meet the lane up to Minninglow. The Parwich lane led up to the back of the farm, and may well have skirted around the buildings before merging with the Minninglow lane. None of these features has been excavated, so the history and character of the farm remain a matter for speculation. Test-pits in the valley bottom, alongside the east field wall, brought to light thirteenth/fourteenth-century green glazed sherds and the

125

85. Daisy Bank: the period 1 barn (?dairy) is in the foreground (photo: Richard Hodges).

distinctive brown manganese-glazed pitchers of the eighteenth century. It is tempting to interpret the meagre evidence to suggest that this site was abandoned in the eighteenth century in favour of the present position. New farms were being built all over the Peak as farmers assimilated the early implications of the agricultural revolution. In its new setting with the farmhouse built into the hillside, not unlike the Romano-British manor, and adjacent to a dewpond, it conformed to a type that W.G. Hoskins has recognised throughout the country (Fig. 86).

The new farm, however, remains an enigma. We can guess with some degree of accuracy what shape it took, but it has not been possible to map its details. Today it consists of a large cluster of buildings enclosing a farmyard. Like the sequence of phases at the Cistercian grange, this farm has passed through many forms in its two-hundred-year history. To interpret these we looked for an archaeological solution – we searched for archaeological clues which did not involve yet more digging! The clues, as it happens, were found not at Roystone, where modern decorations and continual rebuilding left us confused, but at Daisy Bank, the deserted farm on the hill overlooking the valley.

Daisy Bank Farm

Daisy Bank Farm was built in the nineteenth century alongside the railway. Amazing as it might seem, it virtually counts as a prehistoric site, for there is almost no documentary evidence for its history. Now that it is deserted we are dependent upon oral tradition, our own archaeological work and the occurrence of the farm on early editions of Ordnance Survey maps. On the first edition of the OS map, published in 1838, Daisy Bank is shown as Ballidon Moor Barn. It is called Ballidonmoor Barn on the second edition, published in 1897, when it clearly resembles a farm rather than a barn. On the third edition of 1905-6 it is called Daisy Bank, and the buildings look unaltered from the previous edition. The farm was eventually abandoned in the 1960s and, after a period of squatter occupation, it is now used as a hay barn.

At least four different phases of building can be discerned in the remains of the farm.

Period 1

The small south end barn seems to have been the first building on the spot. It is constructed of large, roughly hewn dolomitic limestone and closely resembles a small dairy that used to stand near the Cistercian grange.

Period 2

A single-storey barn was added to the north end of the period 1 barn on the same axis. This had a through passage towards its south end, served by doors in the west and east faces of the buildings. There was also a small square window in the west wall. The doors and windows have roughly-cut limestone lintels.

Period 3

The farm was added onto the pre-existing buildings on the same axis. At the north end is the farmhouse itself with a garden in front of it followed by a stable. Next, the period 2 barn was raised and a first floor was added. Finally, the original period 1 barn was evidently in ruins.

The farmhouse has quoins, lintels, etc. made of gritstone, and its outside walls were plastered with a coarse pebble-dash. The new stable consisted of a stable proper on the ground floor served by a door in the south wall and lit by a window. Above was a hay loft. The period 2 barn had been substantially altered. Not only had it been raised to include a hay loft, but it had been lengthened as well. It looks as though the south end continued to be used as a stable, while the new extension was probably for cattle with a hay loft above. The period 2 east stable door was blocked, but a large window in the south gable wall served the hay loft. This window indicates that the period 1 barn was now without a roof, and quite possibly treated as a high-walled pen tacked onto the east end of the farm. The whole farm sits in its own yard.

127

Period 4

The period 1 barn was restored with breeze blocks, and the south gable window that had been inserted into the next barn was blocked. In 1987, after many years of deterioration, the stone-tiled roof on the period 2 barn was replaced with corrugated iron.

This bald archaeological summary, reminiscent in some ways of our description of the Cistercian grange (see p. 101), needs to be translated into historical terms to be meaningful. In the absence of sound documentary evidence we are reduced to making hypotheses. But, as we shall see, by drawing together several different strands of information we can construct a convincing story.

The period 1 barn clearly pre-dates the railway, and provided the axis on which the subsequent nineteenth-century farm was built. It is not possible to date the barn exactly, but it resembles a small post-medieval cowshed which stood until recently near the Cistercian grange. The barn was located just outside the Cistercian estate, adjacent to a number of fields which were partially laid out in the late sixteenth or seventeenth century but left unfinished. In short, it is probably a field barn built in anticipation of the enclosure of Ballidon Moor (see p. 124). In the eighteenth century lead-miners worked a large rake close to the barn, and it is likely that they used it as shelter in this exposed spot. In much the same way, the period 2 stable may be associated with the enclosure of Ballidon Moor at the end of the eighteenth century. The stable must be the Ballidon Moor barn recorded on the first edition of the OS map published in 1838 – it was in fact a stable with an old barn attached. It is an odd place for a stable, but between about 1830 and 1841 horses were employed on the railway to draw the engines up the steep incline from Cromford. Could the stable be associated with the construction of the railway rather than the enclosure of Ballidon Moor? In view of the fact that there was even more room for stabling in the period 3 farm, there seems to be a good case for proposing that this outlandish spot was chosen for a homestead in expectation of a steady revenue from hiring out horses, rather in the manner of Wells Fargo way-stations. In other words, the farm may have been built after the Ordnance Survey visited the area – probably in the early 1830s – and before the railway introduced full-blooded steam engines in 1841. If this is so, the farm remained largely unchanged thereafter until it was abandoned in the 1960s. Only its name was altered when Daisy Bank Farm, referring no doubt to the moon daisies that grow in profusion along the railway embankment, supplanted Ballidon Moor Farm around the turn of the century.

This interpretation helps us in several ways. First, the period 1

86. Roystone Grange Farm viewed from the site of the late medieval and early modern farm (photo: Ray Manley).

building with its distinctive construction is likely to belong to the first phase of enclosure hereabouts, when the type 2 walls were being constructed. Secondly, an entirely different type of construction was introduced in the nineteenth century with limestone slabs being employed as lintels and sills. Thirdly, in period 3 the previous style was embellished with gritstone quoins, lintels and sills. The gritstone, we can conclude with some confidence, was introduced to this remote place after 1830 when it could be brought by railway.

In the light of this analysis we can now make more sense of Roystone Grange Farm. The farmhouse appears to have been set into the hillside with the barn forming a south wing, and a north wing consisting of a detached stable block. The farmyard was thus sheltered by buildings on three sides. This is how the farm looked when it was first mapped by the OS surveyors in the 1830s. The farmhouse has some gritstone features which suggest that it may have been rebuilt in the nineteenth century. Unfortunately it is impossible to distinguish whether there are older features. The barn, by contrast, seems to be built on a platform revetted by a wall reminiscent of the period 1 barn at Daisy Bank. The building itself has been altered from time to time, but appears to be substantially later-eighteenth-century. The stable block

129

forming the north wing seems to be of a single build, pre-dating the introduction of gritstone features. The eastern side of the present farmyard was constructed before the second edition of the OS map went to press in 1897. This row comprises a pig sty, a large open barn, and a row of stables with hay lofts above. It is unlikely that the range was built all at once, but most of them contain either partition walls or floors made with silica sand bricks that are likely to have been acquired at the Minninglow brick works after about 1860 (see p. 138).

A few other buildings are dotted about the farm. The cowshed by the Cistercian grange has already been mentioned for its resemblance to the period 1 barn at Daisy Bank. This little building has now fallen down, but it was 3.5 × 4 metres in area with a little walled yard alongside it. In many respects it seems to have been similar to building C in the twelfth-century grange complex, and may very well have replaced C when the old farm was abandoned. Access to it was from the grange field, or over a stile inserted through the wall (see p. 38) with steps made from slabs and lintels taken from the grange.

A dairy in the field next to Roystone Grange Farm may have belonged to the eighteenth-century farm, but its present ruinous state prevents us from confirming this. Elsewhere there are two field barns. Close to Jackdaw Rocks, near the Roman site known as Roystone Grange 2 and immediately alongside medieval sheep-pen no. 1, is a large barn with ground floor stalls for cattle and a hay loft above. This features on the first OS map, but it has gritstone quoins, lintels and sills. Like the period 3 Daisy Bank, therefore, we might attribute this barn to the railway age and the intensification of production in the newly enclosed southern parts of the farm. The second field barn, known as Top Barn, lies up the valley to the north of Roystone (Hay Barn 1 in Fig. 29), and again is situated just inside a newly enclosed spread of fields. It is very similar to the first barn and has gritstone features. It also has its own yard, which could of course pre-date the barn. This barn is not on the first edition of the OS map, but it does appear on the second edition of 1897.

As Hoskins remarked, the railway introduced features to these upland farms that brought them into line with village houses. Gritstone features were commonly employed by the seventeenth century in the White Peak, as illustrated by the market hall at Bakewell and the splendid Old Hall Farm at Youlgreave (dated to 1630). With the arrival of the railway, farmers evidently felt compelled to afford the imported stone to keep up with a fashion. As we shall see, they took this to great lengths, even replacing existing limestone gateposts with gritstone equivalents.

'Inclosure ... thou'rt a curse upon the land'

Using the wall typology described in Chapter 2, we can distinguish two main phases of enclosure. In neither case do we have precise documentary evidence for the process. However, the early-seventeenth-century dispute about enclosing Ballidon Moor, described earlier in this chapter, almost certainly relates to the half-completed fields laid out below Daisy Bank Farm as well as other fields. This, we contend, provides the context for the type 2 walls, while the type 1 walls pre-date the construction of the railway and should belong to the late eighteenth century. Plenty of circumstantial evidence confirms this hypothesis. For example, the will of Thomas Leving of Parwich, who died in 1639, makes clear that parts of this parish had been steadily enclosed since the reign of Edward VI. Yet roughly 1,000 acres (380 ha) of common land remained to be enclosed after the Enclosure Act of 1788. Similarly, in Brassington parish there were still 4,000 acres (1620 ha) waiting to be enclosed when the Enclosure Act in 1803 was passed.

At Roystone little of the land outside the Cistercian estate was enclosed in the seventeenth century. But at this time, if not before, many new fields were carved out from the old sheep ranch. The old Romano-British enclosures were re-established, with the eastern wing of the second-century butterfly-pattern being sub-divided into medium-sized fields. New fields were also laid out on either side of the lane to Parwich and alongside the Pikehall-Parwich lane. Finally a small paddock was created at the north end of the meadow in which the farm itself lay. Traces of this wall can still be seen running across the earlier earthworks. The remains of ridge and furrow in most of these new fields reveal that oats and root crops were probably now being grown, as well as many acres of mowing grass for winter fodder. The ranch had been compelled to become substantially more efficient in terms of providing winter feed for the stock. In doing this, the succession of farmers had to come to terms with the shorter growing seasons and harder winters of the so-called Little Ice Age. All in all, there must have been great pressure to find more land to maintain the income of the farm.

The changes to the seventeenth-century landscape were modest by comparison with the complete enclosure of the area two hundred years later. Around 1800 a net of new fields was laid out. Although few new fields were created within the heart of the farm, a tight ring of walled enclosures now spread out to embrace all the high common ground, and extended even to the summit of Minninglow. Surveyors were probably brought in to adjudicate on the line of the new boundaries, much as they were all over England. The lines themselves are often marked out with by fire-cracked dolomitic boulders wedged in place by

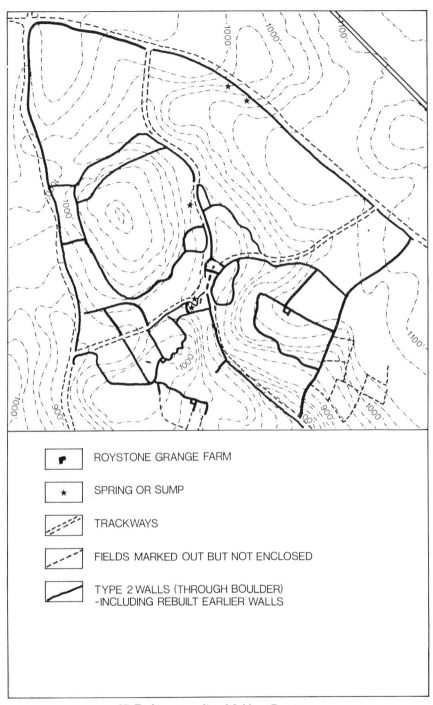

LEGEND

⌐ ROYSTONE GRANGE FARM

★ SPRING OR SUMP

TRACKWAYS

FIELDS MARKED OUT BUT NOT ENCLOSED

TYPE 2 WALLS (THROUGH BOULDER)
-INCLUDING REBUILT EARLIER WALLS

87. Early post-medieval fields at Roystone.

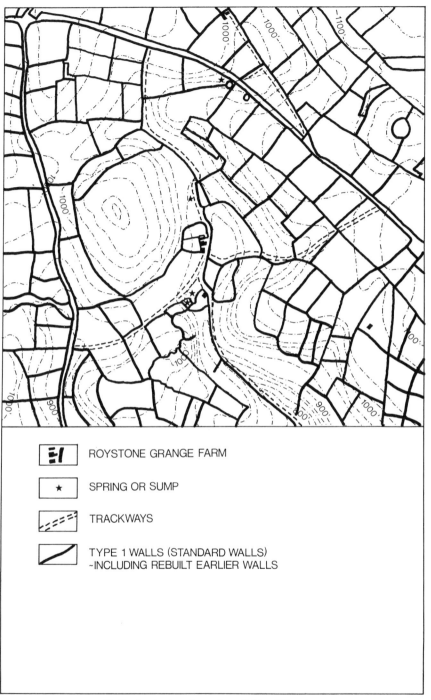

	ROYSTONE GRANGE FARM
★	SPRING OR SUMP
	TRACKWAYS
	TYPE 1 WALLS (STANDARD WALLS) ~INCLUDING REBUILT EARLIER WALLS

88. Early nineteenth-century fields at Roystone.

small stones. This accounts for the abundance of charcoal discovered in the excavation test-pits near the walls. The test-pits also brought to light a considerable number of manganese-glazed pitchers and plates, of which some were doubtless thrown out in manuring, but many may have been broken by the wall-builders. Quite who put up the many miles of walls remains a mystery. Legend has it that Napoleonic prisoners-of-war were drafted in for the purpose. Certainly French officers were on parole in Ashbourne at this time, and several married local girls during their sojourn in Derbyshire. Whoever was responsible, we must acknowledge the scale and organisation of the work.

Unlike their predecessors, these wall-builders used the carboniferous limestone to make their lines across the landscape. Small quarries were dug out in many hillsides to obtain the materials. Thomas Bateman attributes the partial destruction of the cairn at Minninglow to wall-builders at this time. Doubtless some smaller barrows, their cairns exposed by rabbit holes, were completely plundered. Limestone slabs were used to begin with for gateposts and stiles, of which there are several types, as we saw in Chapter 2. Then, in the wake of the railway, gritstone gateposts were introduced. As these were in no way superior posts, we assume that William Webster, who owned Roystone at this time, was influenced by a fashion he had observed elsewhere.

The purpose of enclosure was to increase the productivity of the land. But after a long period of bad summers much of the land was probably in poor condition. Ballidon Moor, for instance, may well have resembled heathland dotted with hawthorn bushes. According to William Farey, who made a survey of the Peak in the Napoleonic age, great emphasis was placed on reclamation to a oats-turnip-grass rotation. Farey reports that heathy limestone land at nearby Newhaven was sown with turnips and subsequently with oats, red and white clover, rye grass and hay seeds. The hay seeds were collected simply by sweeping out hay-barns. In addition, timothy and meadow foxtail grasses were introduced to improve the quality of the pastures. Although timothy is indigenous to the British Isles, it was not until consignments of seeds arrived in England from America in 1763 that it became a commercial success with farmers. The agents of the Duke of Rutland apparently advocated its adoption on their Peakland estates. Other solutions to land improvement included drainage and fertilising with lime. Our excavations within the deserted medieval village at Ballidon uncovered the junction of two fine land drains laid across the deserted medieval village of this time. Channels made of stone rather than terracotta piping were laid down, and were still functioning efficiently when we exposed them in 1986. Many kilometres of drains were laid at this time, echoing out of sight of the historian the great investment made in field walls. No less impressive was the sudden

89. Drystone-lined field drains under excavation at Ballidon (photo: Richard Hodges).

production of lime to produce fine upland swards in the area. William Farey records that '12 to 13 score bushels of lime' were spread on each acre of reclaimed land at Newhaven in the early nineteenth century. Bearing in mind the sheer amount of land enclosed at this time, the quantity of lime involved must have been huge. Great lime kilns produced the fertiliser at Buxton and at Longcliffe (4 kilometres to the east) from about this time. In addition, each farmer built his own furnace. At Roystone a small kiln was dug into the exposed west-facing flank of the so-called Lime Kiln barrow. A pile of rubble beside it shows that a succession of farmers dug out the nearest available stone to feed the kiln. Another kiln lay on the hillslope close to the Top Barn, and a third, well-preserved example, belonging to Minninglow Grange, can be seen beside the railway line, now the High Peak Trail, below Minninglow.

The industrial landscape

It is hard to imagine today, but the White Peak was once covered by the paraphernalia of industrialism. As in South Yorkshire, a great range of industries was practised here among the hill-farms. These undoubtedly created a particular kind of society and atmosphere utterly unlike that of the National Park today.

90. A nineteenth-century lime kiln beside the Cromford and High Peak railway (photo: Ray Manley).

Lead-mining

Lead-mining was the prince of industries on the White Peak. The Romans had explored surface veins for lead, of course, and the monastic proprietors of the region doubtless prospected for the mineral as well. However, the industry appears to have taken off in the late seventeenth century. New building obviously created a demand, as did the need for pipes with the adoption of new standards of hygiene. Lead-mining devastated the landscape. Many fine pastures were irreparably scarred and pock-marked. Perhaps more significantly, with the introduction of steam engines capable of draining deep shafts the mining companies were able to explore veins running far below the hills. In doing so they lowered the water table, and at the same time the lime content of the hills was altered. Furthermore, huge quantities of timber were needed for pit props and for smelting the ore, so many

91. Magpie Mine (photo: Ray Manley).

fine woodlands that had formed throughout the Middle Ages were cut down and, with the poor climatic conditions of the age, failed to regenerate. Most ecologists believe that the present woodlands in the White Peak only began to regenerate after the 1820s as the industry started to contract.

Magpie Mine near Sheldon is preserved as a small, almost pristine memento of this age. Mines like this were distributed all over the region, representing an investment on a par with that in coal-mining in South Yorkshire and tin-mining in Cornwall. It is unlikely, though, that any such mine was ever built at Roystone. Certainly no trace of one survives. Instead, long rakes pre-dating the enclosure walls of the late eighteenth century lie close to Daisy Bank, scar the west-facing slope below the Lime Kiln barrow, and pass down from Roystone Rocks to the meadows below. In addition, small open mines are scattered about near Roystone Grange 2, and several deep openings without any associated spoil were unexpectedly discovered near the Lime Kiln barrow. These operations bear witness to many years of surface exploration, possibly by farmers, or by local companies. It is likely that several stands of trees disappeared with the mining, while a few acres of good pasture near Daisy Bank were damaged beyond recovery. Recently, just after the Second World War, a company returned to the valley to explore a vein running up the near-vertical slope 200 metres south of the grange. In contrast to the eighteenth-century operations this was a clinical job, with much of the waste being taken away for further sifting of the fluorspar.

Sadly, we know too little about how mining proceeded on a farm like this. How did the workings affect the livestock? What terms and conditions were agreed by the farmers and miners? Were the farmers in effect also part-time miners?

Brick-making: Minninglow brickworks

By the late nineteenth century the lead-mining industry was in decline. Many veins had been thoroughly exhausted, while mines in the New World offered new supplies. But the process of industrialisation did not halt. With the railway came the opportunity to exploit bulk resources which could be transported away to the burgeoning new towns of the North and Midlands. The silica sands, contained in pockets between the dolomitic and carboniferous limestone (see p. 14), were such a resource. Bricks could be made from these sands, and with the abolition in 1850 of the Brick Tax − a much despised law passed during the impecunious period of the Napoleonic Wars − brick works were set up in many places along the railway line. In the mid-Victorian period a brickworks was set up beside the railway, close to Minninglow.

The history of Minninglow brickworks, like that of so many industries of this kind, is fairly sketchy. The works do not appear on the first edition of the Ordnance Survey of 1840, but are recorded as working on the second edition of 1899. On the third edition of 1910 the works are marked as disused. Kelly's *Directory of Derbyshire* for 1886, 1891, 1895 and 1899 includes a reference to the High Peak Silica Company operating in the parishes of Ballidon and Parwich. We cannot be certain whether this company owned the Minninglow yard. According to Bulmer's *History, Topography and Directory of Derbyshire* (1895), the High Peak Silica Company was owned by Thomas Wragg and Sons of Burton-on-Trent. The same edition of Bulmer also records that Mr Herbert Biggin of Elton was the works' manager.

The works themselves cover an area of about 0.3 hectares at a point where Gallowlow Lane meets the railway. In fact, the works were placed directly on top of the old lane, necessitating a new route along which the silica sand was brought from a quarry pit about 600 metres away. Two kilns (A and B) lay in the extreme south sector of the compound, furthest from the lane. Immediately north of these were two rectangular buildings (C and D). The western building contained two parts: a rectangular northern section, and in the south a smaller

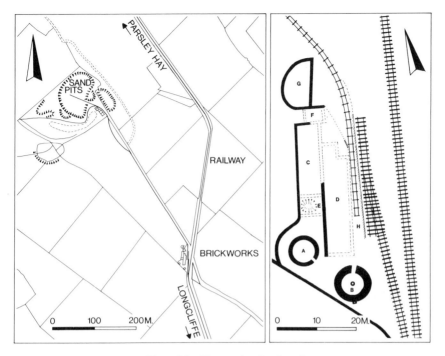

92. Plan of the Minninglow brickworks.

room (E) in which there was a pit measuring 3 square metres. Another building (F) was located towards the northern end of the complex, beside which lay a stone-lined pond (G). The entire compound had been constructed upon a terrace stretching out from the railway, and on its east side a platform (H) also served as the base of the east wall of building D.

Between 1981 and 1986, as part of the Roystone Grange Project, the two kilns (A and B) were fully exposed and a cutting was made through building D. Six periods of operation were identified in the excavations of the kilns.

Phase 1

Kiln A was constructed with an outer shell of shaped gritstone blocks with an inner skin of brick, brick-built flues and a brick floor. The overall diameter was 7.8 metres with a firing area of 5.3 metres served by ten flues in its later phases. Kiln A was initially lined with wedge-shaped furnace bricks, many of which were re-used in the phase 2 floor. Only two features relating to the first phase of operation were found: the brick-built chimney base on the southern margin of the kiln and the circular flue in the centre of the firing area. These features indicate that the kiln began as a downdraught type c. 7.8 metres in outside diameter.

139

Downdraught kilns are characterised by a complex circulation system whereby the air is heated as it is drawn through the fires, enters the kiln and rises until it is drawn down through the centre of the firing area exiting via an underfloor conduit and external chimney. This process was considered more efficient than the updraughting system because the improved circulation of hot air resulted in more even firing.

No indication of either the diameter of the firing area or the number of flues was found. The wedge-shaped furnace bricks used in the later phase 2 floor are probably from the lining of this first phase and do not resemble any other bricks used for lining the kilns, prompting the suggestion that they were specially imported for the construction of the first phase of kiln A.

Phase 2

The phase 1 kiln A was demolished to floor level, the chimney and central flue being filled with rubble. A new, simpler updraught kiln was constructed with an outer gritstone skin lined with yellow standard size building-type bricks. The phase 2 kiln had a firing area of 5.3 metres with the air being heated in ten flues and leaving the kiln via a vent in the roof rather than through the more complex route of its predecessor. The interior skin of the phase 1 wall was stripped away and the best bricks used to re-surface the floor of the firing area. The skin itself was replaced by a yellowish, standard size ($23 \times 12 \times 10$ cm), frogless type of brick.

Phase 3

The inner wall lining of kiln A was replaced. In addition, the floor level was raised by about 12 cm with the addition of large brick blocks set in a yellowish-grey mortar. This time the firing area was expanded from 5.3 to 5.6 metres by removing some of the rubble core in the wall of the kiln. Finally, a woven steel band was bound around the entire kiln, bolted on at several points. The band suggests that the kiln was weakened by the enlargement of the furnace area. At the same time it is likely that the paring down of the kiln walls led to a reduction in heat retention, making it generally less efficient.

Phase 4

Kiln A was stripped of its internal wall lining and much of its floor, almost certainly to provide for the construction of the new kiln B alongside it. Kiln B resembles its predecessor insofar as it had a similar firing area, but it was built with thicker walls and thus had a

93. Kiln B under excavation (photo: Richard Hodges).

greater capacity to retain heat. As in kiln A, a downdraught arrangement preceded an updraught one (phase 5) again with the external chimney on the sourthern margin.

Phase 5

Kiln B was transformed from downdraught to updraught type. The central underfloor conduit was blocked with rubble, as was the external chimney. Presumably a central chimney was now built. In addition, the entrance into the kiln was widened and assumed its present wedge shape. Consequently flue 1 was halved in width. Some of the earlier flooring blocks from kiln B were also removed, trimmed to approximately half their size, and used to support the fire bars in the ten flues.

Judging by the great sheet of vitrification covering the inner wall on its south side, kiln B was abandoned after being damaged by uneven heat. The strong, gusting winds on the hillside might well have caused this to happen.

A third (trial) trench in the brickworks was dug in search of some clue to the function of building D. In it were discovered traces of parallel brick-built walls running north-south. It is difficult to draw an accurate conclusion from such a small excavation, but it is tempting to interpret these walls as the bases of some form of drying platform. In other words, building D may have been used as a drying shed for the bricks before firing.

141

94. Reconstruction of the Victorian brickyard at Minninglow (drawing: Simon Manby).

The history of brick-making is well known. – indeed downdraught kilns like these, built in the 1870s, remained in use until recently at the Loscoe brickworks near Heanor in Derbyshire. On the basis of what we know of such kilns, we believe that kilns A and B were fired periodically rather than continuously. They would have been loaded, fired and left to cool over a period of about ten days. The firing area of each kiln suggests a capacity of 10,000-12,000 standard-sized bricks. If there were three firings a month we might estimate an output in excess of 30,000, and an annual output of about 400,000 bricks.

Several types of brick may have been produced here, but only the standard-sized frogless brick was stamped by the company with the letters HPSC. These were ideal for furnace linings and probably much in demand as industrialisation proceeded in all the neighbouring cities. Wasters were probably used to repair the yard or the railway, while the majority of the yard's output of bricks was despatched by railway to neighbouring towns. A few bricks were used to build the piers supporting the eastern barns in Roystone Grange Farm.

The kilns seem to have had a curious history. Both began as downdraught types and were modified to updraught ones. It is not difficult to appreciate why this happened in kiln A, but why the pattern was repeated in kiln B is altogether curious. The downdraught kiln is the most efficient type: it is easily controlled and, having reached a temperature of about 1150°C, can produce a good finish. It depends, however, upon a sufficiently high chimney draught.

Presumably the exposed situation of the works and the frequency of strong winds necessitated the change to an updraught type. Both kilns had ten stokeholes in their later phases, and both had downdraught chimneys located on the south side. Kiln A had an entrance on the south-east side, while the entrance for kiln B was on the north side, perhaps to minimise the intake of cold air as the fuel was thrown in.

The sequence of alterations to kiln A shows that the company was responding to the needs of a growing market but preferred at one stage to bind the kiln together with a large steel band rather than invest in a new one. Presumably this little industry was under pressure to keep costs down. Expensive new improvements in production technology such as wire-cut manufacturing processes, which speeded up output, obviously put small companies like this at a disadvantage. In later-nineteenth-century Nottingham 24 independent yards coalesced into ten companies in order to take advantage of the new technology. At Roystone the small staff would have been highly dependent upon the skill of the brick-moulder. A good moulder could produce 2,000 bricks a day, so a kiln load for either of the Minninglow kilns would have required 15 man-days. With only one moulder, the kiln could be fired only every 2½-3 weeks, whereas an output in excess of this was probably needed to offset the transport costs. In all likelihood two moulders were employed here, producing batches for firing every ten days or so. The company would also have needed men in the sand-pit, carters to transport material from the sand-pit to the works, and other operatives in the various firing and stacking operations. The cost of employing ten or more people must have made the profit margin very slim indeed. Inevitably, like the small yards in Nottingham, the Minninglow works and several others alongside the High Peak Railway could not compete and eventually closed down. Unlike the lead-mining industry, however, brick-making did not disappear altogether. The quality of the silica sand ensured a market for the sole surviving yard from this age at Friden, 5 kilometres further along the railway line towards Buxton.

*

Roystone figured actively in the mainstream economic conditions that fascinated Adam Smith. Agricultural output expanded steadily throughout the post-medieval period. At first, judging by its new fields, the farm adopted a great variety of agricultural activities. At this time its income was doubtless supplemented to some extent by the lead-mining. Next, it fully embraced the enclosure movement. In the aftermath of enclosure it clearly began to prosper, especially as the railway offered new outlets for its produce. Milk, wool and stock could be loaded on wagons at the Minninglow sidings and despatched to

Derby or Manchester. The population censuses reveal that in the early nineteenth century the rural community in the Peak expanded to meet the new challenges. The new barns, and even the foundation of Daisy Bank Farm on Ballidon Moor, reveal that investment in farming was keeping pace with the changes. The adoption of gritstone for fashionable reasons in the farmhouse and even for gateposts shows that the community could afford to invest in more than utilitarian items. Indeed, the patterned Chinese porcelain, glassware and pitchers found in the excavated test-pits scattered across the farm demonstrate that the products of the manufacturing boom were readily available to people like the Websters. By 1860 the demographic boom had levelled out in the countryside, and with the slow demise of lead-mining some Peaklanders migrated to jobs in the cities. Foreign imports of foodstuffs also introduced a new dimension to agricultural economics. Of course, brick-making, and later quarrying (see Chapter 7) offered new opportunities. At the same time the spirit of Britain itself altered irrevocably. From being a comparatively under-urbanised country with a powerful rural ethos in the eighteenth century, it became a land of great sprawling cities with standards quite alien to the nuclear households working farms like Roystone. This marked the beginning of a great change for the Peakland community. For nearly six thousand years farming had been the pre-eminent national industry, its rhythms providing the guiding rules of society. In Victorian times all that changed, and the urban majority had no natural empathy with the country. From this time, it might be said, Roystone became marginal.

7

An Urbanised Landscape

> That rich undulating district of Loamshire to which Hayslope belonged,
> lies close to a grim outskirt of Stonyshire, overlooked by its barren hills
> as a pretty blooming sister may sometimes be seen linked in the arm of a
> rugged, tall, swarthy brother; and in two or three hours' ride the
> traveller might exchange a bleak treeless region, intersected by lines of
> cold grey stone, for one where his road wound under the shelter of woods,
> or up swelling hills, muffled with hedgerows and long meadow-grass and
> thick corn.
>
> George Eliot, *Adam Bede* (1859)

The fictional village of Hayslope lay near Ashbourne, where 'high up
against the horizon were the huge conical masses of hill ... with sombre
greenish sides visibly specked with sheep, whose motion was only
revealed by memory ...'. Hayslope is champion country, overlooked by
the awesome last scarp of the Pennine uplands. For a southerner, it
offered a haven in contrast to the the bleak treeless region towering
above it. George Eliot's attitude to the Peak District was not new. Nor
did it stem from the steady eclipse of rural society by the growth of
Victorian urbanism. Daniel Defoe, for example, had made disparaging
remarks about the bleak windiness of the region when he passed
through it in the eighteenth century. Some generations later, D.H.
Lawrence, a son of industrialised champion country, was to make
much the same deprecating remarks about the grim 'navel of England'
(see p. 1). In many ways, though, these writers merely echo the
gradual separation of England into two parts: an urbanised lowland
surrounded by fine countryside and picturesque villages, and what we
might call the Other England, where industrialisation was associated
with upland landscapes.

These Victorian images still retain a strong currency today as
politicians debate the existence of a North-South divide. Yet nowadays
most of the Victorian industrial landscapes have disappeared.
Amazingly, abused pastures in regions like the Peak District have
been assimilated into what is now being called the green revolution.
This movement, which embraces such diverse groups as ecologists,

ornithologists and hikers, has its own rhythm, and is quite unsympathetic to George Eliot's division of the countryside. The uplands, as a result, have now become the haunt of the town-dweller. Over 18 million day-tourists, according to a recent survey, visit the Peak District each year, overwhelming the local population of 38,000. Needless to say, farms like Roystone have altered phenomenally since Victorian times. Their marginality became crippling at times before the Second World War, while now, fostered by the Peak Park Planning Board, it is becoming their boon. In the last fifty years governments and bureaucrats have intervened, transforming the landscape into a different resource altogether and severing the long link with prehistory. To be realistic, there is no need to lament the changing circumstances. Yet the landscape is as much a man-made artefact as a natural one, and if we do not appreciate the transition from the industrial era to what we might christen the green age, we will all too easily misinterpret the world in which we live today.

The history of Roystone over the past century sums up the extraordinary changes that have overtaken the uplands of England. In 1894 the Etches family moved to Roystone. They remained there until 1947 when they sold up to the Twigges. The Twigges farmed the land until 1987 when David Twigge retired following the death of his father. At this point, after ten seasons of archaeological excavations, the Peak Park purchased part of the farm and subsidised the sale of the remainder as a historic landscape.

Charles Etches remembers

Charles Etches was born in Roystone farmhouse in 1918 and vividly recalls his first thirty years on the farm. To begin with, the daily 6-mile round-walk to and from Parwich School from the age of 6 made quite an impression upon him. He along with all the children from these outlying farms crossed Parwich pastures and followed the lane down to the village. When he was 12 he left the village school and, like his father before him, went to Ashbourne Grammar. For three years he was a weekly boarder, returning at week-ends. Only snow and hay-making interrupted the educational routine. The former meant week-ends in Ashbourne; the latter school-days missed! When they left school he and his sisters worked on the farm. This was an age before tractors (the Twigges introduced the first tractor in 1948), milking parlours or other machines. The farm depended upon its labour and horses. Besides the family, four or five men helped out, living in the bunk-house above the kitchen. They earned about 5 shillings a week, as well as their board and keep. In addition, Irish migrant workers came by in late June and helped for a month with the hay-making, before setting out for Peterborough to pick peas and potatoes. By 1940

95. John Etches and his wife
(courtesy of Charles Etches).

they were paid £2 per week each, but slept in the hay barns. As a rule the Etches had 27 horses on the farm, of which ten were used for working. Two were shire stallions which were almost always out servicing mares all over Peakland. Roystone shires earned a great reputation, and Charles Etches still retains the name as a prefix for the horses he shows as a hobby in national competitions. The horses were well-treated, and when a favourite mare named Polly and another called Roystone Speedwell died in 1928, John Etches had them buried in the grange area (as we discovered: see p. 106).

Before the advent of EEC quotas Roystone was alive with stock. There were only 100-150 sheep, a quarter of the size of the Cistercian flock, but there were often 30 dairy cows, 70 beef cattle, 10-12 pigs, 20-30 geese and a good number of hens. The cows were milked by hand beside the pond in the farmyard until the Ministry of Agriculture condemned the conditions in 1947. The geese were kept in a close that included a small mere opposite Lime Kiln close until a few weeks before Christmas when they were driven back down to the farmyard to be fattened up. The ganders apparently defended them against foxes. The hens, too, were kept up in the fields – in a pen by the old Lime Kiln. Besides stock, over a quarter of the farm was given over to crops. They grew oats, turnips and potatoes and had nearly 100 acres under mowing grass to support the stock through the long winters. Besides

96. John Etches and his shire-horses in the 1930s (courtesy of Charles Etches).

domesticated animals and crops, they made use of natural resources. There were incredibly large numbers of rabbits before myxomatosis was introduced after the war, and they undeniably over-grazed parts of the farm. They were easily caught, however, and every autumn the young men set up wire 'hangs' to snare them. Charles Etches recalled trapping 58 in one evening. The were usually sold locally, though during the war they were bought by butchers from Sheffield. In 1948, David Twigge recalls, a rabbit fetched as much as 1 shilling. In autumn, too, there were mushrooms to be collected which also fetched a fair price at market.

But this diversity of stock and crops was no guarantee against hard times. A free market existed in the 1930s, which favoured the great farms of Australia, New Zealand and South Africa and disadvantaged hill-farmers like the Etches. Often during this period, Charles Etches remembers, his father would accompany the 8 o'clock train with his milk to the dairies at Manchester to ensure its sale. Having left the milk with the co-operative he would proceed home, only to find a telegram at Roystone telling him that they were returning the milk. On occasions he travelled as far as London to sell his milk. When there was no buyer and the milk was even rejected by the co-operatives making cheese at nearby Brailsford, Grange Mill or Hartington, Mrs Etches herself turned it into a Derbyshire Stilton. Wool, too, did not sell well during this period. More than once they had several years' fleeces stacked up in the pump house. Roystone's days as a sheep ranch were truly over by this time. In search of spare cash, the Etches sometimes quarried stone on the land and sold it to the County Council for road-making as the old lanes of the White Peak were surfaced with tarmac.

In many ways it was a very self-contained life, but one brimming with activity. John Etches always rose at 5 am to begin the milking and went to bed at 9 pm. When there was grass to be mowed, he was up at 4 am and out until the light faded. Life was not all work, though. Every Thursday the family went to market 8 miles away in Ashbourne. This was the real day out, and involved a ritualistic round of heavy drinking in the pubs before the horses found their own way home. The farmhands tended to visit the Sycamore in Parwich for a drink, while Charles Etches recalls long walks to dances all over the district. Often on a Saturday night he would follow the railway line to Longcliffe and then cross to Wirksworth for a drink. On other occasions he rode to dinner-dances at the New Inns near Alsop and even the Peveril-in-the-Peak at Ilam. The Parwich wakes were also a time for a good deal of fun. The wakes began on the last Monday of June, so every year John Etches would begin the hay-making on the Saturday. He never worked on Sunday, being church-warden at Ballidon. Then on Monday the family would join the merriment in Parwich. First they would walk round all the big houses where they were liberally oiled with beer. This was followed by a heavy, long lunch in the Sycamore. Next there were fairground amusements to take in, as well as more drinking to be done. Each year, therefore, the mowing began in earnest on the Tuesday with the household nursing heavy heads. Even so, still more liquor was on hand. Cutting a hundred acres with a scythe was hard, punishing work. Their thirst was slaked by beer in gallon flasks, many fragments of which turned up in the test-pits. It was always said that 14 gallons of beer were required to help mow the field known as 14 Acres!

Next in the agricultural calendar was a month spent removing the thistles. Following this the threshing machine arrived from Cubbley. It was drawn the 15 miles or so by a traction engine and travelled to all the White Peak farms in turn. Each farm supplied a man to help for the season. For two or three days it would stay at Roystone, and here as at each place on the engine's circuit the farmer's wife, in this case Mrs Etches, would serve up huge dinners for the hands. Each September the Etches drove their stock to the Newhaven fair, held on the grass verges beside the road. At about the same time they visited the Hartington fair, which dates back to the early thirteenth century. Then in October there was the Oldhaven fair at Newhaven. These were occasions to hire new hands, to find a new sheepdog and to sell surplus stock.

In autumn an occasional day would be spent shooting partridges. In poor years the Etches let the shooting rights to businessmen from Derby. Then there was ploughing to be done, interrupted only by the

97. The pumphouse at Roystone, which provided air for the pneumatic drills used in the quarries visible on the skyline (photo: Ray Manley).

intervention of the hunt. In bad winters such as 1947 the Etches hired themselves out with their horses to clear snow. With spring, as the cycle began again, there were fields to be fertilised. Lime bought from the Alsop Moor kilns was deposited in piles on the land and then spread with a shovel. Basic slag bought in Ashbourne was also used. Spreading this was a foul job, often as not given to a man they wanted to get rid of. The slag was carried up in a hessian sack tied to the back, and distributed by hand from a hopper tied to the waist. The poor person was certain to end up dusted in ash. However, Charles recalls, it made the clover shoot up.

In the spring of 1939, shortly after the Munich crisis, the Conservative government paid a subsidy of £1 per acre for ground that was ploughed up. With this act the long tradition of farming here changed. During the Second World War and thereafter, successive governments offered more subsidies, and eventually, with British membership of the EEC, the government introduced farm quotas and effectively became instrumental agents in formulating the agrarian regime at Roystone. The Etches were not unhappy about this. All the uncertainty about whether the milk or wool would sell finally came to an end. Charles Etches remembers watching the bombers fly overhead

150

98. The round-roofed explosives hut at Roystone (photo: Ray Manley).

towards Sheffield, and the distant thumping of their bombardment. A bomb even landed at Pikehall.

Farmers were not the only people affected by the changing rhythms of twentieth-century life. Just before the First World War a quarry company purchased several acres of ground near the railway. Stone was needed to maintain the expansion of industries in the nearby towns. The first of these quarries, beside the railway, was served by a siding. A second, on the slope overlooking the farm, was meant to be served by a tramway leading up from Lime Kiln close. The tramway was completed and the quarry opened up, but fortunately for the landscape here it was quickly abandoned, though not before it had removed half of Roystone Grange barrow 1. The first quarry, however, was worked throughout the 1920s. Pneumatic drills were now used, powered by air pumped up from engines in a pumphouse beside the Cistercian grange (Fig. 97). The pumphouse was built here, far from the quarry-face, to take advantage of ample supplies of spring water to cool the cumbersome engines. No one seems to know why it was built in the style of a large Nonconformist chapel. Another building of this age is the round-roofed explosives hut (Fig. 98). The little reinforced alcove contained the explosives used in the quarry. The door was reinforced and a notice issued by Imperial Chemical Industries spelt out the details of the 1875 Explosives Act to the quarrymen. Section 82 of the Act, so the notice informs us, warns that a fine of up to £2 will be made upon anyone defacing or removing the notice. The hut is of a type well-known from naval dockyards in Edwardian times and quite out-of-place on this exposed hillside. Still, it was a good place to have lunch, Charles Etches says, when they were out thistling.

Up to thirty quarrymen were hired in Parwich and walked the 3 miles to the farm via Parwich Meadows every day. Much of the work was manual with hammers and wedges. Some days the gang of men were fully employed, whereas on other days only a certain number were needed. Charles's father John often employed the unlucky ones in exchange for a meal.

Like so many industries, the Roystone quarry ceased operation during the depression of the 1930s. But in 1945 the Ballidon quarry was opened up. The original quarry lay on the east side of the gorge, at the point where the White Peak scarp ends. The Etches found the new quarry a profound nuisance. Invariably, on returning from Ashbourne, they were held up at the bottom of the valley by lorries queuing to be loaded with stone. So, after almost 54 years here, John Etches decided to sell up.

Ralph Twigge's farm

Ralph Twigge bought the farm in 1947. He was born in 1893 on a farm at Atlow near Ashbourne, where his father specialised in raising horses. Ralph Twigge went to school with John Etches's younger brother, and before the First World War frequently visited Roystone. He often commented that there were always so many people sitting down to supper at Roystone in those years that an extra one wasn't noticed. As a young man he accompanied his father to Ireland to buy horses, making the journey there and back on horseback. Many of their horses were sold to the Oxford and Bucks Light Infantry, and so with the outbreak of war in 1914 Ralph immediately joined the regiment. Like so many he could not have imagined his fate. He survived the Somme, where he was gassed and then shot in the neck, and ended up at Sidcup in Kent in a convalescent ward. He decided to buy a farm there, and for almost thirty years the Twigges worked a series of farms around Canterbury. However, when the University of Canterbury compulsorily purchased their farm just after the Second World War they decided to move back to Derbyshire.

David Twigge, recently demobbed from the RAF, joined his father on the farm. He was paid £2 per week, his board and the profits from all the rabbits he could catch and sell. But life at Roystone did not return to pre-war conditions. The government was concerned to make Britain self-sufficient in food after the war and offered many incentives to help the Twigges. The Ministry of Agriculture sent farmhands with a disc-plough to cultivate the high pastures, so that a regime of rape, kale, oats and grass could be introduced. The Ministry also introduced

99. Ralph and David Twigge
(courtesy of David Twigge).

them to making silage. The Twigges themselves brought the first tractor to Roystone. In 1948 they installed piped water and cattle troughs in place of the meres. Soon afterwards they had electricity. At this time too a new dairy and a corrugated iron hay barn were erected just north of the farm beside the Romano-British homesteads. And when David married he had a cottage built for himself. The planning authorities gave him a choice of location for the new dwelling: the platform on which we found the twelfth-century grange or a spot opposite the Top Barn, far from the farmhouse. He chose the latter because he felt that the grange field was too damp and dark!

Not everything changed, of course. Oats, potatoes and turnips were grown as before. Cows, cattle and sheep grazed the hills. Work-horses were used too, though their numbers dwindled steadily as tractors replaced them. The Irish migrant workers still called each hay-making season, and the markets and fairs still brought some respite from the demanding routine. Only one train a day, though, now ran along the railway. And for the first time an occasional hiker ventured up the lane, heralding a new era. Hikers were drawn by the new National Park, founded in 1950, and as early as 1945 could take advantage of the Whitemeadows youth hostel at Ballidon, run by Mrs Taylor. From Whitemeadows, so the 1945 YHA Handbook tells us, it was 7 miles to the next hostel at Hartington, 2½ miles to a small one at Brassington,

153

100. David Twigge shearing in
1986 (photo: Ray Manley).

and 6 miles or 6½ miles respectively to those at Elton and Wirksworth.
Whitemeadows had the capacity to accommodate up to seventy
hostellers, but evidently it did not prosper and by 1958 it had been
closed.

The farming community altered swiftly over the next twenty years –
more rapidly than at any other time in its history. Increasing farm
wages lead to fewer farm-workers and more mechanisation.
Nevertheless, subsidies offered some compensation. At the same time
new strains of barley and grass were introduced that could survive in
the upland conditions. By the 1960s the Twigges could afford a large
corrugated barn, which was put up in Haybarn Meadow, and a
combine harvester. However, Roystone's circumstances were irrevocably altered when in 1967 Mr Beeching on behalf of the government
axed the Cromford and High Peak Railway, and the National Park
turned it into a trail for walkers and cyclists. More and more people
were beginning to gaze down into this concealed valley. Britain's
membership of the EEC heralded the beginning of the end. Hedged
around by subsidies and penalties, Roystone like all Peakland farms
was encouraged to favour dairying for some years, then beef, then
sheep. This chopping and changing to meet European needs
accelerated cycles experienced over much longer periods by the
Twigges' Romano-British and medieval forebears. In the hands of the
unscrupulous such policies can imperil the landscape itself. Not that

101. Along the High Peak Trail towards Minninglow (photo: Ray Manley).

this happened at Roystone, where Ralph and David Twigge tended the ground, wary of the new fertilisers and skilful in managing their stock. But inevitably, with less labour at their disposal, fewer acres were ploughed, silage increasingly replaced hay-making, and thistles invaded many meadows.

When we chanced upon Roystone Grange in 1978 Ralph Twigge had retired. We were truly fortunate to discover David Twigge, for he may be one of the last generation to remember farming when it involved an uncomplicated relationship with the landscape and elements. He respected this spirit and allowed us to appreciate how his distant forebears would have managed here. For ten years we profited from his experience. With great generosity he allowed us to roam the farm digging holes and exploring the history of the place. He also encouraged the creation in 1984 of an archaeological trail between the monuments, which drew new visitors to his world.

The trail begins at the Minninglow carpark, once the sidings to which several generations of Roystone farmers took their milk each morning. It follows the railway for 2 kilometres, past a small quarry and a fine lime kiln, to the brick works described in Chapter 6. From there the trail branches off along Gallowlow Lane beneath Minninglow itself until it reaches a footpath that maintains a prehistoric, Roman and medieval trackway down to Roystone itself. The farm comes into view after passing beneath the High Peak Railway, as does the Lime Kiln barrow on the promontory to the left. The trail winds down to the

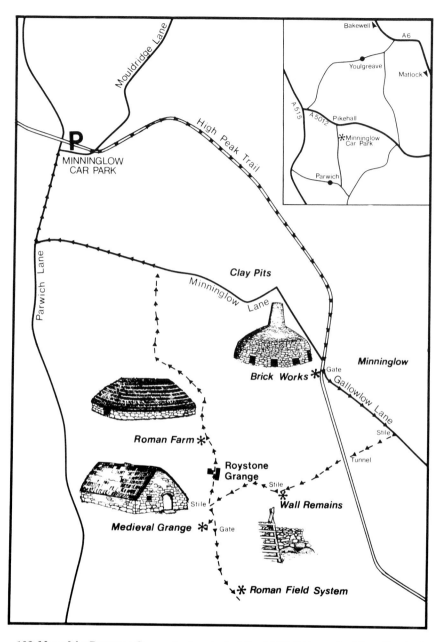

102. Map of the Roystone Grange Archaeological Trail (1984) (drawn by Diane Tranter).

156

Bibliography

Reports on the excavations and surveys at Roystone Grange will be published in archaeological journals. Interim reports and essays have already appeared on the barrow cemetery, the Romano-British village, the grange and the Minninglow brick works in the *Derbyshire Archaeological Journal*.

A readable and authoritative introduction to the region is Roy Millward & Adrian Robinson, *The Peak District* (London, 1975). For the ecology see P. Anderson & D. Shimwell, *Wild Flowers and other Plants of the Peak District* (Ashbourne, 1981). Barry Marsden has written a short biography of Thomas Bateman entitled *The Barrow Knight* (Shipley, 1988) from which many of the details used in this book are taken. Of the many studies of British landscapes, the following are recommended: Andrew Fleming, *The Dartmoor Reaves* (London, 1988), W.G. Hoskins, *The Making of the English Landscape* (London, 1955) and *Fieldwork in Local History* (London, 1967), Christopher Taylor, *Village and Farmstead* (London, 1982), Oliver Rackham, *The History of the Countryside* (London, 1986), and Tom Williamson & Liz Bellamy, *Property and Landscape* (London, 1987).

Studies of walls are especially rare, but see Arthur Raistrick's classic *Pennine Walls* (Leeds, 1946). On the prehistory of the region see John Barnatt in the *Derbyshire Archaeological Journal* 106 (1986) and *Proceedings of the Prehistoric Society* 52 (1987). Note also John Collis, *Wigber Low* (Sheffield, 1983), Clive Hart, *The North Derbyshire Archaeological Survey* (Chesterfield, 1981) and Jeffrey Radley's numerous reports in the *Derbyshire Archaeological Journal* throughout the 1960s.

No useful modern synthesis of the Romano-British archaeology in the region exists at present. However, Derrick Riley, in *Landscape from the Air* (Sheffield, 1980) offers a view of this period in the regions to the south and east, while K. Branigan (ed.), *Rome and the Brigantes* (Sheffield, 1980) covers the region to the north. Note also Leslie Butcher's surveys of Romano-British sites in the *Transactions of the Hunter Archaeological Society* 12 (1983).

On the later Roman and Anglo-Saxon periods see Richard Hodges, *The Anglo-Saxon Achievement* (London, 1989). The Ballidon charter is published by Nicholas Brooks, Margaret Gelling & Douglas Johnson in *Anglo-Saxon England* xiii (1984). Granges are well-surveyed in Colin Platt, *The Monastic Grange in Medieval England* (London, 1969). See also his *Medieval England*

159

Bibliography

(London, 1978) for a sound guide to the period and its archaeology. Enclosure and open fields are discussed by R.A. Butlin in H.S.A. Fox & R.A. Butlin (eds) *Change in the Countryside: Essays on Rural England, 1500-1900* (London, 1979). On the farm itself see R.W. Brunskill, *Traditional Farm Buildings of Britain* (London, 1982). Lead-mining is concisely described in Trevor D. Ford & J.H. Rieuwerts, *Lead Mining in the Peak District* (Ashbourne, 1975). For the origins and development of the National Park see Roland Smith, *The Peak District National Park* (London, 1986). Finally, a guide to the Roystone Grange Archaeological Trail is available from the Information Offices of the Peak District National Park.

Index

Index